D1600110

IN ASHANTI & BEYOND

A Kussasi Actor.

The slayer of a buffalo, he re-acts the hunt at public gatherings. The cowrie bedecked horns, however, are of wood and are not the original ones.

IN ASHANTI & BEYOND

The Record of a Resident Magistrate's many Years in Tropical Africa, his Arduous & Dangerous Treks both in the Course of his Duty & in Pursuit of Big Game, with Descriptions of the People, their Manner of Living & the Wonderful Ways of Beasts & Insects

BY

A. W. CARDINALL, F.R.G.S., F.R.A.I.

District Commissioner, Gold Coast

Author of "Natives of the Northern Territories of the Gold Coast," "A Gold Coast Library" &c. &c.

With Illustrations & a Map

NEGRO UNIVERSITIES PRESS

WESTPORT, CONNECTICUT

Originally published in 1927
by Seeley Service and Company, Ltd., London

Reprinted 1970 by
Negro Universities Press
A Division of Greenwood Press, Inc.
Westport, Conn.

SBN 8371-3285-1

PRINTED IN UNITED STATES OF AMERICA

AKWADA! AKWADA!
AI YE!! AI YE!!

FOREWORD

SO fast are times changing in what one used to look upon as Savage Africa that I do not think it necessary to offer an apology for publishing notes taken at random concerning the passing ways and passing people of the Gold Coast. I have spent most of my time in lonely stations, in districts where no other white men reside, and most of my interest in my people has been roused by watching the lives, at work and play, of my boys. It is difficult to realize here in England how much these latter mean to one. Actually they are as much friends as servants, faithful and loyal. To them—especially to Kojo Num, who died last year after giving up to my service his country, home, friends and life—I must record my thanks. For they have instructed me and have given me much interest and pleasure; and it is mainly of what they have shown me and taught me that this book is concerned.

A. W. C.

SEVENOAKS

CONTENTS

Contents

LIST OF ILLUSTRATIONS

IN ASHANTI & BEYOND

CHAPTER I

THE GOLD COAST

IT is curious how the tropical parts of the world appeal so strongly to the romantic side of most Englishmen's imagination. There is the Spanish Main with its pirates and gold, buccaneers and Holy Inquisition; there is the East with the wonderful John Company nabobs and their untold wealth, mutinies and tea clippers; there are the South Seas, lands of head-hunters, cannibals and blackbirders. But the West Coast of Africa stands second to none in this realm of romance. Guinea! The very name itself speaks of gold coins, slaves and spices—pirates as well!—mangrove swamps, fever, fetish. The very miasma of malaria enshrouds the coast with the mystery of the unknown.

And what inspiring names have been chosen for the various parts of the Guinea Coast: Grain Coast, Slave Coast, Ivory Coast, Gold Coast, Pepper Coast! Moreover, did not our fathers recall to us, or do we not ourselves remember, Cape Coast Castle, whence Wolseley started on his march to punish blood-soaked Coomassie, or later still the massacre of Benin?

So it was that when I was appointed to the Gold Coast I could not but conjure up these images impressed in boyhood on my brain. I am afraid, however, that, as is so frequently the case, boyhood's impressions and beliefs were roughly proved erroneous. One should never grow up.

I do not think that I actually believed I should meet slaves and massacres, nor yet stumble on vast quantities of ivory and gold, but I certainly expected to meet fever and fetish. I had learned before my departure, in a course of lectures and instruction one must attend before definite appointment, that the fever miasma was a myth, and that the less romantic mosquito—the word "gnat" takes away still more idea of romance—was responsible for most of the ills of West Africa; and so vanished too the deadly miasma of the mangrove swamps.

But what is the Gold Coast? In official publications we find it is an arbitrary name given to a three-hundred-mile stretch or so of the West African Coast, and contains a certain amount of interior country. The name itself is probably the oldest of these local European names, and is due to the fact that here particularly was gold-dust brought to the coast for barter with the early merchant adventurers from Portugal, Holland, France and England.

The actual area of the country known to-day as the Gold Coast amounts to some ninety thousand square miles—a very minute piece of the continent of Africa. It is divided into three parts: the Gold Coast Colony, Ashanti, and a Protectorate which suffers under the lengthy title of "The Northern Territories of the Gold Coast." The last is by far the greatest in area of the three, whilst the second is the best known on account of its notorious past. In addition, a small portion of the former German possession, Togoland, is, under mandate, included in the various parts of the country.

But the Gold Coast is comparatively little known even to-day, in spite of its extraordinary wealth in natural resources. Being a purely arbitrary name, which together with the name Ivory Coast alone survive of these former regional divisions of the Guinea Coast, it very inaptly describes the country, now that gold has almost ceased to be an outward sign of wealth. Authors in the past have searched for other names. Ellis recalls the romantic with "Land of Fetish"; Eiloart would be unpopular to-day with "The Land of Death"; and Mr Dove is perhaps too commercial or American when he christens the country "England's Richest Crown Colony."

Personally I like "The Land of Death." If everyone called this country by that name what a hero I should be, even in my own family. It would be useless for Governments to proclaim "The Land of Death" an almost health-resort; chambers of commerce could not countenance the rapid opening up of a country so called, even if the name were a recognized misnomer. I doubt if staid investors would care to lend their money to such a country. But just imagine one saying good-bye to acquaintances in one's club, and a prompted friend asking carelessly: "Where are you off to this time?" And then one's ready reply: "To 'The Land of Death.'" In any case, that name sounds more attractive than the sobriquet given to Sierra Leone, "The White Man's Grave."

I do not intend to discuss whether West Africa is

healthy or not. Everyone knows that tropical countries are not as a rule suited to Europeans, and the question of the healthiness of a country such as the Gold Coast is a question of fact, not argument. One has merely to collect statistics, such as the number of those who entered the Gold Coast Service in a certain year, how many are still in the Service, how many draw pensions, how many resigned before pensions were due, and how many are dead. If one did that—say, from the year 1900—one would learn facts which no solid arguments could refute.

But all men know the reputation of the West Coast of Africa. Therefore, when one is appointed to a post there, the Government wisely takes care to see that officers are first carefully instructed in the elements of tropical hygiene. Lectures are given which all must attend, and there one hears all about terrible things like *spirochætæ*, *flagella*, *filaria*, and other awesome and awful beasts which the tropics seem to foster.

One therefore proceeds to the West Coast in a humble and chastened mood, hoping that matters are not quite so bad as they are painted, and half reassured that it is the other man who will " peg out " anyway. In such a mood I embarked at Liverpool, bound for the first time to the Gold Coast. Sekondi was my port—the steamer labels spell it Seccondee, but orthography in place-names is never over-strict. I had not heard of it before, but a map informed me that it was the railway terminus for Coomassie, with which name I had long been familiar as the town of human sacrifice, fetish trees, kola (a so-called portrait of Prempeh in an illustrated paper of 1896 showed that monarch in process of chewing one—needless to say, it was a picture that the licence permissible to artists alone can excuse, for it is inaccurate in every detail), and wonderful umbrellas. I knew I was bound for Ashanti, so presumed I would reach that famous spot.

My timidity as regards the climate—not in its meteorological sense, but in its generally accepted and wider meaning, which covers weather and its effects, either direct or indirect, on health—was not exactly lessened during the first voyage. A West African liner is unique, I should say, among liners, for there are no passengers on board who are tourists or pleasure-seekers. Soldiers, merchants, miners, missionaries and officials make up the passenger list. Conversation is therefore chiefly West African shop, and new-comers are, perforce, listeners. Invariably the conversation will turn on the departed—it is a trifle dangerous to discuss the living—and once one mentions one who has died then everyone remembers others, and so the grim list is gone through, and the wretched new-comer grows more and more miserable.

There were several of these on board, so we formed our own little set and refused to listen to the horrible old-timers, or pretended not to believe them. This pretence was not very strong, however, and when off the African coast, in murky, sultry weather, with a river-stained sea that smelt of decay, the limit to my sufferings was reached in a piece of tinned caviare.

Now there used to be a delightful custom in West Africa, and on its steamers, known as "small-chop." This was a kind of *hors d'œuvre* served at that time of sociable conversation during the hour preceding dinner, when the sun has sunk below the mainyard, and drinks, long and short, pass round. I wrote "used to be." To-day the advent of so many ladies has almost exterminated this pre-dinner session, and their innatc economy will not tolerate this tax on the store cupboard and on the kitchen. But on my first voyage small-chop was regularly served (it is being revived on the steamers again), and one night we had tinned caviare.

Next day, after a night of pain, none of us felt very fit, and I was leaning over the rail, sorry for myself, hating the sultry dreariness of the seascape, and in a mood to believe the worst of all things. By my side was a nursing sister who already had done many tours in West Africa.

In order to cheer myself up a bit I innocently remarked to her: "I suppose the Gold Coast is not really so bad as it is painted?" She turned on me and almost screamed: "How dare you suggest such a thing! You've never been there! You know nothing about it! It is far worse than it has ever been painted." I think she also must have had some of that caviare.

As I turned away to find the purser, in order to induce him to give me a return passage on tick, she repented and muttered: "But if you take your quinine regularly perhaps you will be all right."

Now quinine is a most unpleasant drug. One never seems to get quite used to its flavour, but one had learned in London that it was a sure defence against malaria, and that regularity in taking it was essential. I think the lecturer had said something about deafness, and possibly idiocy, probably weakening of the brain, surely loss of memory resulting from its continued use. I tell you, West Africa was made extraordinarily attractive.

On this my first voyage I had heard much about quinine in the smoke-room, and of all the stories told there I have never forgotten this one as an example of the terrible result of quinine-taking and its resultant loss of memory. I do not think it has appeared in print before, although it is a well-known West African yarn, and moreover true:

"Yes; it is extraordinary how the stuff affects your memory. You know N.?"

"Oh, rather! He is about due to retire now, isn't he?"

"Yes; he went out last boat on his last tour. He and I came together. Well, he had heard somewhere or other that a hippo-hide made a most excellent table-top; and last tour he slew a hippo on his way down from the north. He had the hide more or less dried before he came on board, and it was stowed forward, and for some reason or other on deck. What with the sea air and general dampness that skin became undried, and by the time we left Sierra Leone it was very noticeable. Its noticeability became more and more pronounced, and we all begged N. to have it thrown overboard. But he is an Irishman, and out of sheer cussedness refused to part. A petition to the 'old man' was equally unavailing, and we had to seek refuge aft in the smoke-room.

"Eventually we reached Plymouth, and we all, together with the undried and very whiffy skin, went Londonward. I did not see N. when the train reached town, but met him in Liverpool the day before he sailed.

"I asked him how he had got on with his skin, and whether the table was a success. And he laughed. 'Extraordinary thing, old man,' he said, 'I lost it.' I pointed out that that was almost an impossibility, as the smell alone would betray its whereabouts.

"'Well,' he replied, 'the fact is I did lose it. You remember there was a bit of a rush when we got to town, and I was in a hurry. I gave the skin and some boxes to a porter to look after, and he gave me a receipt for the boxes. The skin was still on his trolly, and he said he could not leave that in the cloak-room as it was a bit ripe, but suggested a sort of lamp-room place where he assured me it would be quite safe. Next day I sent for the boxes, but did not bother about the skin until I had fixed up with the people who make skins into tables. That was two days later. They gave me a man to collect the skin, and we went off in a taxi from the shop to the station. Nowhere could I find that lamp-room, nor could I locate the porter. I rather think I created a scene, as lots of people, apparently important, came up and argued and apologized and all that sort of thing. Anyway, the skin was not there, nor did anyone remember anything about it. Of course I did not know what time I had arrived, nor by what train; I merely knew I had landed at Plymouth. So having got very angry, and having told everyone what I thought of them, their trade union and their railway, I apologized to the shopman, and to avoid trouble with the police I left Waterloo in a temper.'

"'Waterloo!' I said to him. 'Why, man, you arrived in town at Paddington!'"

Now there is an example of loss of memory which

obviously must be due to this quinine idea of the doctors.

The logic of this last remark is open to discussion, but its effect on one just recommended to take quinine regularly—that is to say, five grains every day and often ten for the next twenty years—was not encouraging.

However, it was all refreshing and new. I had seen quite a fair portion of the world, but nothing quite like this first West African boat. The voyage itself needs no description. Almost everyone takes a sea voyage nowadays, and they are all more or less alike—to some monotonous, to others interesting and all too short.

One's first impression of West Africa, though, is certainly unexpected. Sierra Leone is usually the first port, for one does not quite reckon Dakar in French Senegal as true West Africa, but rather belonging to what, on the map given at the back of the Elder Dempster passenger-lists, is called the "Land of the Moorish Tribes."

Sierra Leone is the original "White Man's Grave." One expects something in the way of scenery, one does not quite know what, to accord with such a significant name. But, instead, one steams into a magnificent bay, with forest-clad hills and delightful sandy coves and lagoons. A white lighthouse set among palms is at the very entrance, and a short distance in front lies, and has lain for many years, the wreck of s.s. *Fulani.*

I used to envy the lighthouse-keepers. It looked a healthy and pleasant job, and I thought of the wonderful opportunities they must have of collecting moths with their powerful light. A Sierra Leone doctor informed me the other day that many of these men are invalided home with lung trouble, which was believed to arise from the dust of the scales from the moths' wings.

On one's first voyage one ought to go ashore at Sierra Leone. There is really nothing to see, but it is quite an experience, and for the first time one feels horribly shy and self-conscious of one's colour. The market, too, with its wonderful variety of colour, fruit and vegetables, skins and clothes lying all anyhow on the stalls; the variegated head-dresses and blouses of the women, the babel of noise, the heat and the smell, all make up a scene not soon to be forgotten.

But it is not likely one will repeat the visit.

Freetown is too damp and hot, and one sees the same elsewhere on the coast.

Generally the steamers manage to get away quickly, and then proceed south and westward along the coast, which, according to season, is kept in view or not. The run along the coast is not remarkable once the hills of Sierra Leone have dropped below the horizon—a low-lying, tree-clad coast, with now and then a silver beach and immense surf-breakers of a dazzling white; a sea that is no longer blue, but stained brown and red, and even green, from the many rivers; a sticky, lifeless breeze.

One passes Monrovia; but even if one calls to drop a passenger or two, there is no time to go ashore; and finally one reaches Cape Three Points, a really wild seascape of rugged rocky headlands and breaking surf. Sekondi is in sight, all green and red and white, a typical tropical sea-town, the red cliffs surmounted with the green of the palms and shrubs and undergrowth, and the glaring white roofs of the houses strikingly crowned with a square white building, Fort Orange, lighthouse and jail. But it is West Africa; and what is quite a pleasant sight is spoiled by one of the ugliest buildings man ever created, the Wesleyan Church. That is real West Africa. Everything somehow gets spoilt.

CHAPTER II

"BOYS"

STEAMERS arriving at Sekondi lie off a good distance from the beach and one has to land in surf-boats. All this will soon be changed, and one will step ashore down a gangway just as is done in the prosaic docks of Europe. Another of the romantic side-plays of West Africa will have gone. It is all commonplace enough, this surf-boat landing, but to the new-comer it is always a mild adventure. A surf-boat is merely a long-boat with paddlemen instead of oarsmen. One does not usually walk down a gangway, as the swell is too great, but is lowered into the boat by the derrick in a "mammy-chair." This is a kind of sea "victoria" with the doors removed, and only a foot or so of weather-boarding in their place. It is a novel experience being slung over the ship's side and rapidly lowered into a boat, where ready hands receive one. It looks dangerous: it is certainly awe-inspiring; but accidents rarely occur. Once I was watching a nursing sister and a young man being lowered. The chief officer had just explained what a wonderful derrick he was working, all done by electricity, fool-proof and perfectly safe, when something went wrong, and the chair went down with a rush. The surf-boat just got clear, and the two occupants of the chair were for a moment completely immersed. I turned to the chief officer. He had fled to the control man, and as I did not wish to embarrass him (the control man was in sight) I withdrew.

Once in the surf-boat, seated in a Madeira chair, one begins rapidly to notice the heavy swell, and is generally quite glad to see the half-naked paddlemen take their seats along the gunwales, insert the large toe of the right or left foot in a rope-sling, and commence to paddle in time with a weird barbaric chant. All this is quite up to expectation; and the curious three-pronged paddles resembling sharks' teeth, and the song, which is just pure doggerel, combine to make landing at Sekondi quite an adventure. Add to these the surf itself, great white-capped breakers tearing shoreward.

Sekondi is far better than most places on the Gold Coast. But even there it can be bad. When the harbour at Takeradi is completed, yet another of West Africa's romantic experiences will have gone!

The day I first landed, the surf-boat was run up on the beach, and before I knew what was happening two burly men had seized me, most painfully under the arms, and I was more or less thrown ashore—very surprised, but quite dry. To-day the surf-boat is replaced by a steam-launch—a Gilbertian affair, but quite businesslike —and one steps ashore on a prosaic iron grating and climbs to a quay up an iron stairway.

What a landing that first one was! Everybody knew one was a new-comer, and a vast swarm of "boys," would-be servants, thrust into one's hands their credentials, or those borrowed from their friends. All these hundreds of "boys"—some were grey-haired—wanted to be engaged, either as one's valet, or butler, or cook—steward, boy and kuku are the West African terms.

Now this is a very serious business, this engagement of boys, and I will return to it later. Sufficient is it that I engaged none on the beach. I had made a friendship with an old hand, who, as it turned out, accurately forecast all my movements, and he had promised to engage one for me, saying that later on one would get a second "boy" easily enough.

I therefore waved them all aside and made my way towards Allen's Hotel, where another friend had engaged a room for me by cable from Sierra Leone. On the way thither I saw the bank. Excellent idea! I would cash some notes. I entered, and whilst conversing with the cashier fellow the manager himself strolled round. He greeted me most affably, asked who I was, whither I was bound, and in what capacity. I told him. He asked if I was opening an account with them, and when I said "Yes," he asked, to my profound astonishment, "Can we accommodate you with a small advance? Often you fellows are short." He was quite apologetic about it. And for the first and, I hope, only time I refused an overdraft, and to cap it all I asked him to come along and have a drink. I must explain I was used to American ways—that is, before she went dry.

Anyhow he agreed, and conducted me into the bar of Allen's Hotel, where we met Mr Allen himself. Then for the first time I met officialdom, not in its bad sense, but in its purely formal meaning. We had our drinks, and I told Allen that I was staying with him. He begged to differ, on the grounds that some other arrangement was sure to have been made.

Allen was right, and soon a young-looking man arrived and fetched me away. So I left Allen's and gave myself into the hands of this official, who conducted me to the Provincial Commissioner. He was kindness itself. I was a raw hand, and he did everything for me.

We gathered in an empty bungalow, and during the course of the evening a " boy " arrived with a note from my friend saying he thought he would suit. That was my first boy—George of Lagos. It is an interesting subject, this of boys. In Lord Edward Cecil's *Egyptian Memories* are some delightful paragraphs on " boys." Summarized, they are to the effect that there are boys *and* boys ; most of them are useless, rascals and thieves : those of one's friends are nearly always in this class, but, curiously enough, one's own boys are exceptionally excellent, trustworthy and loyal.

It is very much the same in West Africa. One can first of all class boys into two divisions—those in the service of men stationed in towns or headquarters, and those in the service of men in bush and lonely stations. The former come to one fully apprenticed, alien-trained ; and it is a mere toss-up as to whether they are good, mediocre or bad. The latter come to one when they are untrained—mere children ; and they stay often until the end of one's service. These one learns to love and in them lies no fault.

Now George was my first boy. He was about twenty years old, extraordinarily ugly, full of life and apparently of humour. He stayed with me four months, and water unfiltered and not boiled was his end.

Meanwhile he had been joined at Sunyanî, whither we had gone, by one Kwami, a nice, very tall Ashanti youth. He robbed an old lady in the market of her eggs and then, when stopped, smashed them on her head. His departure was, I think, to him somewhat painful.

Then a little schoolboy attached himself to my household out of school hours. He was Kofi. He bribed his way into my family by bringing me four eggs, laid by his own fowls. He just sat on the floor of the house and smiled and produced the eggs. I took them, and he joined the staff. But in just over a month I left Sunyanî, and he remained at school.

George and I went alone to Goaso. There the Commissioner whom I was to relieve was running an excellent house. He had, to help his head-boy, two children from the village. I thought I should like to do the same. The evening before he left I pointed out a likely child, and he arranged with its mother. That child was Kojo—or, to give him his full name, Kovo 'Num, being the fifth child. He became my boy, friend more than servant.

Everything then was so novel. There was not too much work and I had plenty of time to devote to my household. Kojo was very quick, as most of these children are, and soon learned to lay a table, clean up, make a bed, and all that sort of thing. He had one peculiar trait at that time, and that was to take off his cloth when at work, whether waiting or at other jobs, and do it naked. He was very frightened one morning at a sudden sneeze of mine which caused "goose-flesh," when scores of white spots suddenly appeared on my sun-red neck and chest. He pointed at me in terror, give a shriek and fled into the bush.

Kojo was joined by two friends, Kobina Bona and Kwami Amankwa. The former—steady-going, rather slow, but faithful and most lovable—stayed with me till he died, four years later, at Zuaragu. His last words were really terribly pathetic. He was delirious, and evidently was arguing with his mother, who did not wish him to accompany me to the north, for he clearly said: "No, mother, I will not stop at home. I will go with my master." Two days later he died—but he never spoke after those words, which were clearly said.

Kwami Amankwa was never quite on the permanent staff of my household. He used to come round now and then, give me a francolin of his own trapping, or a fish, help for a day or two and then go off again. His pay varied from one shilling to four shillings a month. He came to me afterwards at Prestea, stayed a month, and then expressed a desire to go to school. So I sent him to a commissioner friend at Coomassie, where he went to school and did odd jobs in his spare time. He is now in the police and doing well.

Then came big, overgrown Kwesi Donkor. I do not quite know how he came—"He just got there." He did not want to leave Goaso, and when I left he did not follow me. He meets me now and then in Coomassie, and we exchange news. He is the proud possessor of a double-barrelled gun, but uses a flint-lock one to kill birds or animals. I remember him best over an incident at Dadiasoaba. We had trekked in from Mahame, only four miles or so away, and Kwesi had forgotten a kettle. I told him to go back and get it. Later I saw him going from hut to hut in the village, and I naturally inquired what he was doing. He explained that he was going back to Mahame, but he was afraid of the pixy-folk (*mmoatia*) in the bush, so he was just looking up a companion. I asked him if he had ever seen one; and he gave me a detailed account of one he had met, and their conversation, and all the ills he had met with afterwards. He found his companion and they saw no pixy-people.

But before Kwesi came I had lost George. He was never overclean, but when, after warnings, he deliberately gave me water that had neither been filtered nor boiled, I really could not do otherwise than send him away. I was then cookless. But my corporal, now a superintendent of police, came forward and helped out for a week. He made most exquisite loaves and cakes. He was an Ashanti man, and a great friend to my two children-servants, Kojo and Kobina. They had once thought, or known, that George was taking more than they considered right; so they went to the corporal and he brought them crying to me, two naked little boys, attached to either of his hands, and told me that they were not thieves, but that some of my sugar and jam was going. As a matter of fact, native children in the bush detest jam and sugar at first, and have to break themselves into the taste, just as we do with whisky.

The corporal was succeeded by the court bailiff. That was Kwami Boi. He preferred a safe income to the haphazard one of fees and commission. He too was an Ashanti, and he stayed with me nearly four years, when he left, on account of continual sickness—but only when he knew I had found a substitute. He had guinea-worm in both ankles just before he left, but he insisted on going. He was afraid to die in the far north.

At that time my household consisted of Kwami Boi, Kojo Num and Kobina Bona—all Ashantis. It was a very happy family. Then Kwami left. A week later Kobina died. But Kojo refused to go and braved the ill-luck out. In no spirit of disdain may I use the term spaniel-like devotion, which these boys have? When one lives, as I have lived, entirely alone, for months together, without a visit from another white man, one learns to love them, and perhaps they learn to love one too.

Kwami was succeeded by Salifu, a Moshi man. His career is an extraordinary one. He was the son of the Chief of Beloussa, a grandson of the Na, or Sultan, or Emperor of the Moshi, which is the most important negro kingdom in all West Africa. He was a small boy when the French in 1896 took Wagadugu, the capital. They at once set up an effective administration, and decided to send chiefs' sons to school. Now Beloussa is the second in rank to Wagadugu itself, and the custom was then that every son of the Wagadugu chief, *ipso facto*, was a chief, and by their diligence, bravery, wealth, etc., rose in rank until they became chiefs of Beloussa, and then Bassuma and, finally, Wagadugu itself. Now Salifu's father was a son of the Na, and therefore, having reached the grade of Beloussa, was in the direct running to become Na himself. Therefore the French wished to collect some of his children to educate them. But Salifu and his brothers thought, as also they had been told by their father, that they would either be eaten or sold as slaves by the white man. They ran away, but were recaptured and put on a steamer, probably the *Mage*, the first on the Niger, and were to be taken to Say. But they again escaped, going ashore on the pretext of buying food, and made their way to Wagadugu. There they met — from Salifu's account—Voulet himself, the conqueror of Wagadugu. He was very kind to them, gave them plenty of food, and even ponies. Eventually they went over to Diebugu, apparently for education. They were all quite happy, when H.E. the Governor of the Gold Coast Sir Matthew Nathan arrived on the frontier to inquire, or assist in the inquiry, into the death of a British soldier on the Black Volta (Salifu's story). The French officers entertained His Excellency, and as a means of entertainment set these Moshi princelings to racing. Salifu attracted the Governor's eye and was persuaded to accompany him to Accra, where he did odd jobs about the castle, and became His Excellency's jockey.

Some time after that, Sir Matthew Nathan left the country, and Salifu was given a long letter to the French at Wagadugu. Everywhere he was assisted. He left Accra, in the company of a doctor, for Sekondi and Coomassie. Thence he was given five carriers to Kintampo and thence to Wa and Tumu, when he left British territory and came to Leo and Wagadugu. But unfortunately Salifu had washed his trousers on the road and had left the letter inside them.

The French officer could not decipher the pulp, but recognized Salifu as of the blood royal of Moshi, for no man, under penalty of death, save he be a king's son, dare bear the facial mark denoting that rank. It is a cut on the left cheek from the bridge of the nose to the middle of the cheek. The ordinary three cheek-marks of the Moshi are there as well. He did not know what could be in the letter which Salifu declared was from the Governor of the Gold Coast, and sent him back to get another.

Salifu returned via Bawku and Zuaragu to Coomassie, where he entered the service of a transport officer. His adventures did not cease. He successively became boy to a soldier, to another doctor, and then to one who took him north again to Say and right across to Dakar and down to Sierra Leone, where his master stopped. Salifu continued to Sekondi once more, where he met his second medical-officer master and again entered his service. That was in the yellow-fever outbreak of 1910.

But, at some period or other, Salifu was at Sekondi when he met a friend, one Kwesi of Sansane Mangu. This man told Salifu that his master wanted to take a lot of boys to Europe. So Salifu and some friends went to interview him. They found a man with "a belly that reached from here to right over there. When you sit down here, the belly reached to there [six feet at least] but his foot was so small!"

Salifu then went to England, working on the steamer. For a month they stayed at Liverpool, when they all returned to Southern Nigeria, together with the fat man. Here they met the late Boyd Alexander, and they left the fat man, who proved to be a German, and made one trip with Boyd Alexander, whom they left on his way home at Sekondi, where Salifu rejoined his medical officer.

Salifu then found a new master, with whom he stayed for some time. The war broke out and Salifu accompanied his master to Togo. He was then left with his master's wife, and when she went home to England he accompanied the late Captain Butler, V.C., to the Cameroons. Captain Butler went home and Salifu went back to Zuaragu, when he entered my household.

That is a fair example of a "boy's" wanderings. It is extraordinary how mindful they are of detail—but of chronological order they have not the least idea. Salifu is still with me. He engages from time to time what he terms nautically a "cook's mate." These I rarely see and hardly ever know their names. Eventually they become cooks and drift southward into the service of other men. If this practice ceased there would soon be no cooks at all on the coast.

Of all these apprentices of the kitchen one only is known to me. He is Asubiri, and he ought by rights to be a cook by now. But he is a Fra-Fra, and with all the tenacious loyalty of his tribe refuses to leave my service, and is still content to receive a pittance of fifteen shillings per month.

When Kobina died, a number of unremembered small boys came and went until Kojo introduced the Snake, one Awafo, the son of my next-door neighbour at Zuaragu. He earned his name from being born shortly after his father had escaped from a python. Kojo had apparently attracted him, and he served as his horse-boy, then my knife-cleaner, and at last became an excellent servant. He was given by me to a great friend, with whom he still serves.

Awafo's peculiarity was never to laugh. He could smile, but it was a very disdainful smile, and I think he looked on all of us white men as beings to be pitied and helped.

He in turn introduced a small boy—one, Akansaki, or "I refuse"—which was an excellent name for him. When Awafo had gone he began by being a very good boy, but got into evil hands. Our parting was a very painful one to him.

But there were many others, who just passed through the range of my vision. There was Jatto, who explored a bicycle tyre's inside with my hunting-knife. A stirrup leather was, I think, the last thing he noticed in my house. Then there was Simpowa—Threepenny-bit. He chose that name for himself. His real name was rather less modest. It was Awambajiggi. When asked why he chose "Threepenny-bit," he replied that that was the amount of money his master had first given him! I trust I shall not be blamed by Child Labour Protection Societies for my apparent meanness.

Simpowa was quite an interesting child. He came to me entirely of his own accord and asked for no man to introduce him. I had had a meeting with the chief of Sandema, and was standing by the cairn of stones erected to the memory of those who gave their lives to their king in 1914-1918, when a small naked boy touched my hand and smiled up at me. I grinned back and greeted him as Chief of the Chicken Hawks, and asked him if he had any complaints.

"Do you not remember me?" he queried. I had to reply "No"; whereupon he reminded me that we were friends, that the last time I had visited Sandema—some eight months before—I had awarded him a penny for his marksmanship with a bow and arrow. He had then slain a small bird within a given time-limit, and had presented me with the booty. He now declared his intention of entering my service. Kojo was willing; so he entered the family circle.

Next morning he was missing, but joined us on the march, naked, but on his head a small packet, which he informed me was his clothing. About a week later we were in Navaro, when I saw a lady holding the flag-pole. This was the usual practice for anyone who wished especially to see the Commissioner. The next step was for the D.C. to send a boy—anyone would do—and ask the complaint. There was no need to hear the answer. One merely told the suppliants to go to the court and wait; which they invariably did, quite satisfied. One then heard their woes later with correct interpretation. It is rather fine to think of the flag as a house of sanctuary, and one cannot but conclude that one's predecessors were gentlemen-adventurers all.

I sent Kojo, and he came back and told me it was Simpowa's mother. I told her to go and have some breakfast in the kitchen and I would see her later. Simpowa was apparently indifferent, and was more than usually busy; the plates all clattered more, and he ran out and back quickly, gave frenzied rubbings to the knives, but paid no notice at all to "mother."

After breakfast I interviewed the lady. She said her child had just run off without a word, that someone had said he was with me, and so she had come to see. I showed him. She then said he was too young. I gave her two shillings, and said she was a good mother to come all that way—seventeen miles—and why not leave the boy, anyway, until I got back to Sandema. Simpowa meanwhile was paying not the slightest notice. He was too old to bother about women, I suppose. He was at most eight years of age.

Anyway the lady agreed to my proposal and went home. A month later she came back, and I saw Simpowa on her lap, playing and laughing. He had given her a shilling, and she was very happy. She told me that the boy was fatter than if he had stayed with her, and she would be pleased if I would keep him.

This love for mothers is very pronounced. It is always so perfectly natural—as it should be. I used to give Kojo a cloth at the end of each tour, when we reached Coomassie, and until his mother died he always asked if he might give half to his mother. Akansaki too, rascal that he was, likewise gave his mother half his pay.

But to return to my boys. Kojo, of course, was the major-domo, and on this last tour, when to my irreparable loss he died, he brought me a small Ashanti cousin, one Kofi Simma, a bright, intelligent child. But Kofi was an enigma. When Kojo died, Kofi shed no tears, and only broke down a month later, when Kojo's brothers arrived and sent him to buy palm-wine for the funeral custom. Kofi left me, naturally enough, when those brothers returned to Goaso.

CHAPTER III

THROUGH THE BUSH TO SUNYANÎ

MY second day on the Gold Coast was in the train. The two other new men, George and myself embarked at an unearthly hour in the train bound for Coomassie. It all seemed cruelly modern. I knew Coomassie from pictures of the 1896 war—Coomassie of blood, reeking sacrificial trees, vast heaps of skulls, pictures of weird, wild dancers, all the romantic imagery of savage Africa—and here was I in a prosaic train, with a ticket of pasteboard naming Coomassie as its licensed goal.

But there was romance enough at the station. Noise unspeakable: shouting, conversation, laughter, officials of the railway rushing about—probably flushed, but not visibly so—shouting orders, countermanding orders, in English and vernacular; policemen in blue shorts and puttees, with blue uniform and red fez, but unmistakably policemen, as their sleeve bands showed, ordering people about, pushing them into the train and hauling them out; and one perspiring European, either stationmaster or engine-driver; but whatever his job he seemed, in spite of his obvious heat, to be set above all this din, this fantastic clash of colour. One could see that at least he was going to get the train off on time. Then the colour. I have called it fantastic—that indicated the shades—but as for the actual choice of colour, nothing could have been more in taste. Reds and yellows and greens, sober blues and browns, fezes and turbans and white caps of the chef pattern, rags and tatters, silks and fine cloths—they all were in harmony, perfectly suited to the people, the place and the sunshine. The only jarring note was some European-clothed people who had not the education or bearing to carry such unsuitable clothing. Ye gods, how ugly are our European clothes!

Somehow everything was sorted out and the train started. What a journey that was! The line made every possible turn and twist; the wheels on the light rails emitted ear-piercing shrieks; the engine puffed and grunted; the heat grew more and more oppressive. Eleven and a half hours of discomfort and noise. To-day the rails are heavier, the shrieks have gone, the turns and twists have been straightened out, and the run reduced to ten hours—an average of just over sixteen miles an hour, but not too fast for the egregious tsetse if one is foolish enough to leave a jalousie lowered.

But at each station there was interest and amusement enough and to spare. Hundreds of people rushing about, shouting, apparently all bewildered with excitement. Colours magnificent. And, most striking of all, everyone was laughing, and happy. A passenger, bound no matter whither, seen off by all his family, proud to travel by train, and they proud to be related to so important a fellow. Everything was a joke. People passed my window and smiled up at me in sheer *joie de vivre*. I grinned back. I began to like West Africa. I have learned to love it since.

Then there were the women-purveyors of food: roasted plaintains, loaves of sweet-tasting bread (palm-oil used to raise the loaf), unknown food matter packed in loaves, smoked fish and smoked snails. Oh! it was all novel, and in sheer sympathy with my fellows I grew happy. Look at those cakes, just like dough-nuts. How appetizing they look! Then the girls with water, a liquid not fresh, but full of flavour no doubt. But how well they carry themselves, how well they have chosen the colour scheme of their apparel! And their smile, the flash of the teeth! Then the children, all naked and dusty, but fat little lumps of happiness and insolence, and certainly of fear.

Then into the midst of all this chaos strode the engine-driver. He knew all about it, saw it every day, and all that he cared for was to see that his prosaic, modern, glum train started on time. He walks into the station-master's room, checks the time, gives a curt order, his guard whistles, a bell clangs, everyone shouts, the train puffs and snorts, the wheels and rails squeak, and we scream and shriek for another hour, when the same scene is repeated.

But what of the scenery? No ordered fields or meadows, no trim, ugly smoke-crowned roof-tops, no dusty roads nor rushing telegraph-poles. Just jungle and forest, a wild mass of greenery with extravagantly coloured flowers, palms and ferns. Giant white-skinned trees, looking as naked as skeletons, straight for two hundred feet or so and crowned with branches out of all proportion to the foliage they bear. Trees, all flower-bedecked—scarlets and golds and whites; trees grotesque and ill-shapen, with their startling white trunks and fantastic buttresses;

palms, some magnificent, others untidy; others without their crowns and fire-stained; bushes ablaze with colour.

Now and then an eighteen-inch-wide path, mysterious and fascinating, inviting one to explore its route, minute amongst its cyclopean surroundings. Now a village: huts leaf-roofed, with walls of yellow stucco and sticks; scores of naked boys, all laughing and waving to the train; babies trying not to be afraid, but at last tearing away to the shelter of their houses or elder relatives.

It was one vast image of luxuriant life. Here and there a sluggish pool, or maybe rivulet, which burst volcano-like into a fairy display of winged colour, disturbed by the train's vibration. Butterflies of hues enough to drive an English schoolboy mad with zest to capture and destroy—greens and violets, blues and scarlets, yellows and whites, large and small—the long-desired happy hunting-ground of every youthful entomologist.

I shall not soon forget my first voyage northward in a Gold Coast train. To-day it is a little altered: one has become blasé without doubt, accustomed to all this riot of colour and clamant life; but, more than that, the railway is straighter, makes less noise, and the forest is cleared back farther from the line, so that the jungle which has replaced it soon wearies one with its monotony, save, perhaps, where blazes the gorgeous poinsettia, which tradition quite wrongfully says is scarlet only in Ashanti—vermilion from the blood of the sacrificed. Perhaps an Ashanti of to-day would resent that extravaganza—five hundred years hence he may be proud of it.

There were only three halts that impressed themselves on my brain: Tarkwa, Dunkwa and Obuasi. Tarkwa had two or three smoke-stacks of iron—a mining camp obvious to the veriest tyro—its natives not so artistically clad, but with dirty white or khaki trousers and caps—poor imitations of Liverpool African firemen. Tarkwa had also its ordered villages or camps, the most prominent feature of which were the bath-houses. Dunkwa—just on the Ashanti border—provided but one impression—that of sawn logs, all weather-worn till they were a nondescript blue-grey, probably two feet in diameter and twelve feet long, but all of extreme value—mahogany. They looked just like Douglas firs which had been long exposed.

Then came Obuasi, with miniature mountains, bungalow-crowned and double grass-crested. Later I saw an English lawn and beautiful roses in the mines-manager's compound. Obuasi is the great Ashanti gold-mining centre, and is a cosmopolitan (in so far as Africa is concerned) township, well ordered and clean. It was particularly impressed upon me by an unlooked-for kindness. At that time the Commissioner used to be informed, at his own request, of what passengers there were on the north-bound mail train, and he gave those of his own department, as well as others, most refreshing tea, sent down to the station. This, like "small-chop," is now a thing of the past.

I spent a week-end at Obuasi once. My host and hostess were charming, and immune to their pet sand-flies. This immunity was not shared by me. Since then I prefer to have nothing to do with that city; but I shall not forget the really fine display of roses in the mines-manager's and Commissioner's gardens. The two men were rivals in horticulture, and with the exception of a garden at Tarkwa these were the best roses I have seen on the Gold Coast.

By the time the train left Obuasi one had grown very tired, dirty, deaf, sticky and thirsty. Coomassie, therefore, an hour and a half later, came as a great relief. The railway station was quite a good building; to-day the terminus has been shifted, and unexpectedly has become a fine building.

But I was so tired when I first stepped out of the train at Coomassie that my impressions were but dim. The Acting Chief Commissioner was on the platform where our coach stopped. He had come down to meet a fellow-passenger from Liverpool who was bound for the northern protectorate, to whom he introduced me, and I was asked to stay at the Fort.

This was the historic Fort where, in 1900, a gallant stand was made against almost overwhelming hordes of the Ashanti. It had become the Residency, and is endeared to many by the memory of much hospitality, joviality, kindness and sympathy. Coomassie was, when I first came there, like a big family; everyone was kind, and vied with each other in hospitality and friendliness to the stranger who was passing. Time has altered this, and Coomassie, like other towns, is too occupied with its own society to worry about mere casuals. The old tradition is preserved only in the mess of the Gold Coast Regiment, which naturally enough is centred here. One cannot expect it to be otherwise; but most of us are in our hearts conservative, and regret the onward march of progress—*alias* mercenary materialism.

A terrible thing occurred here at Coomassie during my first night. For the first time I found I had to play bridge. I had escaped hitherto; but excuses were impossible, so I was roped in and forced to succumb. For four hours I sweated blood. I knew the game, but only as a rather interested critic; now I had to play. Shortly after midnight my torture was over. I had lost my partner and myself half-a-crown.

The Acting Chief had told me at the station that I was to go into the "bush." My second day was spent in getting advice, persuading the Transport Officer that I really did want to go, making one or two official calls, opening an account with one of the trading firms, promising the bank to do likewise, and in the evening walking with one of the nursing sisters around Coomassie.

This was very disappointing—almost as bad as one's first visit to Chinatown in Vancouver or San Francisco. I do not know exactly what I expected; but whatever it was it was not there. Coomassie was then, as it is to-day, a Europeanized native village, as large as a small town, with cleaner streets and alleys and empty spaces than one would find in any Mediterranean country. As a matter of fact, I have seen nowhere on the Gold Coast such filthy streets or disgusting habits as in Naples, in 1920 and 1924. The Ashantis are remarkable for their extreme cleanliness; and they take a pride in themselves, their clothing and their houses, which some of the other tribes do not, and many of the non-African population completely ignore. But Coomassie, which in 1896 was

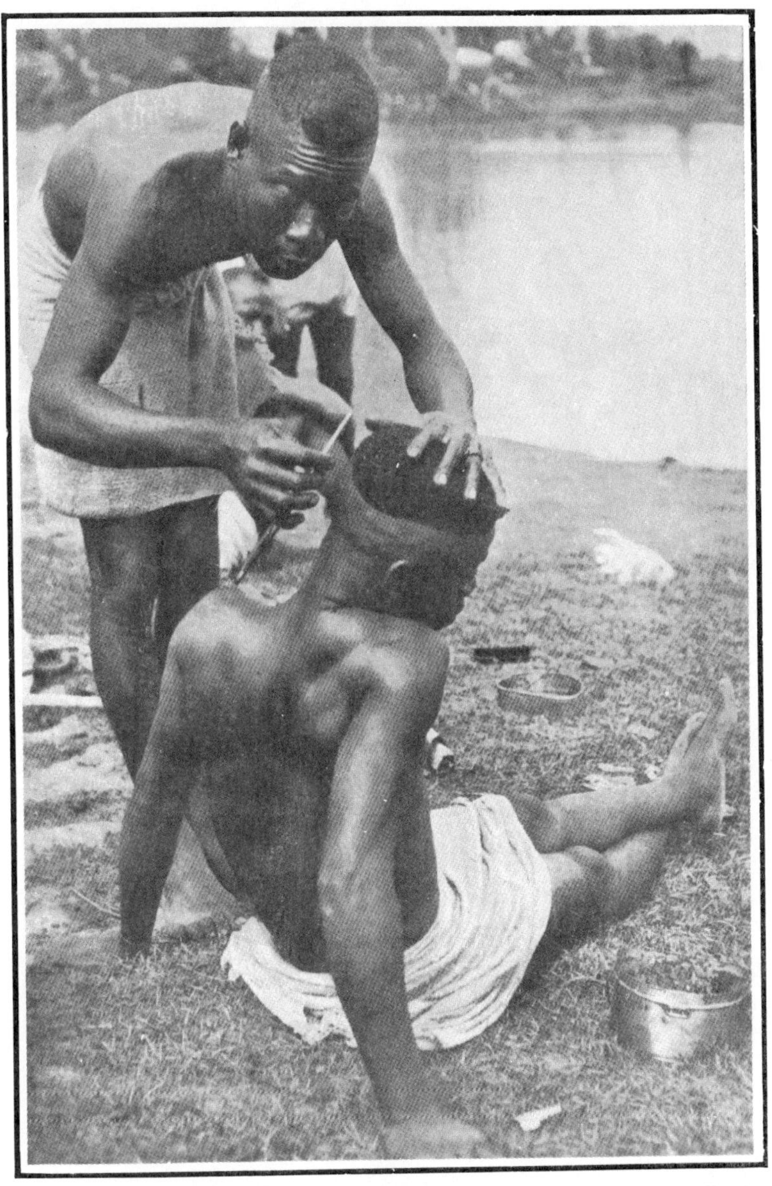

HAIR-CUTTING.

Two Dagomba carriers cutting each other's hair. In this case a European razor is used: usually it is of native make. The hair is cut and shaved in all sorts of patterns.

described as reeking of human blood, crying aloud for the hand of the cleaner, was scarcely native at all when I saw it.

Next morning my carriers, or porters, as earlier writers were wont to call them, arrived; my loads were taken out of the Fort and distributed without a sound by an old lady—one Mariama—who had the carrier business almost as a monopoly. To most men who know West Africa such a thing as a silent distribution of loads on the first day seems almost an impossibility. It is usual to see pandemonium, chaos. Apparently everyone is about to fight everyone else; curses seem quite ordinary; vicious winding of clothes into a pad for the head look like menaces; the cook, the steward, the escort all cancel each other's instructions; the headman and each carrier shouts his opinion and advice. A wise man walks off in the direction of that day's destination. His carriers will pass him in ten minutes or so, laughing and joking, as happy as can be, running along, and that with the prospect of a twenty-mile trek, carrying sixty pounds on the head all the way!

There is an end to all things, even to one's carriers getting away while one is looking on. Thus mine departed, so did George. Then I turned back to say "good-bye" and "thank you" to my host. He came out smiling and wished me luck, and added words which are of priceless value: "Remember always to salute the Ashanti first. You are above them. They think so anyway; and they will not greet you unless you bend from your height to them. If you don't do this, you will think them surly and unfriendly."

That was one of the finest bits of advice I ever received. It rather shows the topsy-turvydom of negro thought, but it is not applicable to the negroid protectorate northward of Ashanti, where the peasant greets his superior first.

So I left Coomassie, and for six days wandered along a woodland track—hammock-road we call it—towards Sunyanî. I forget how many carriers I had, but there were eight hammock-men. That was quite a novelty, and I funked getting into the hammock.

Hammocking is to-day almost a thing of the past; therefore a description of what was an everyday affair in that not-distant past may not be amiss, though hard. A hammock is some eight to nine feet long. There is a ridge-pole, to which are fixed cross-pieces, whence hangs the hammock. If one takes the precaution to have plenty of cushions, riding in one of these contraptions is by no means uncomfortable; but the bearers must be trained to break step.

That first trek of mine through the forest was disappointing. The train journey had led me to expect mightier trees and more gorgeous flowers, but I found the forest less dense, less lofty than those in the coast ranges of Oregon or British Columbia. The only striking objects were the rich redness of the soil and the myriads of gorgeous butterflies massed together at every puddle; whilst the noise of countless frogs—a very Tower of Babel in the batrachian world, in which every species and every batrachian dialect were represented—made night if not hideous at least not lonesome. From time to time the chorus of frogs and crickets would cease all of a sudden, only to be renewed with greater vigour when the danger, or whatever had caused the silence, had passed. The first night, too, there was the occasional awful shriek of a child in agony from some devil-begotten torment—merely a tree-bear calling to its mate. On later nights one was no longer so much disturbed, until one eventually became so accustomed to the noise that sleep on board the steamer, when going home, was impossible because of the stillness.

The villages one passed through, though naturally novel at first, were all very similar to each other. The Ashanti likes to have one broad street, along which the houses are irregularly set. These usually consist of four rectangular, single-storeyed rooms, either with a verandah or quite open, facing on to the central yard—a familiar enough type throughout the Mediterranean coasts. The side streets are merely paths, sometimes almost impassable owing to the roofs being so low and almost touching. These are of grass, of palm leaves, and of a leaf from a variety of arum. Wealthier people have shingle roofs—wooden tiles made locally; and the really well-to-do even go to the extent—*horribile dictu*—of corrugated iron. One day someone will, I hope, make proper tiles—the clay is excellent and timber fuel not difficult to obtain

This Ashanti type is quite characteristic, and lends itself to development. The houses devoted to the custody of the altars and shrines of the gods are often decorated in stucco mouldings, somewhat reminiscent of Egyptian and Eastern scroll-work. The mud, or, as we call it, "swish," lends itself to easy handling, and excellent arches can be made, as well as filigree- and trellis-work.

Moreover, the style of building—with its central yard—is eminently suited to tropical climates—far more so than the introduced style of European bungalow, or the tumble-down patchwork hovels for which the African in the West Indies is, I think, responsible.

Without incident I reached Sunyanî. I arrived on a gala day—the opening of the new Government school. There were five white men at Sunyanî, and when I arrived they were all at the school. Of this I was informed by the postmaster, and just then received a note to go down. I arrived. As I entered the children began to sing, and everyone stood up. I felt very shy, albeit flattered. But I had made a bad break: they were singing *God Save the King*—but I have no ear for music.

For two months I stayed at Sunyanî. To me it was an interesting time. There was my first case. I was in the office one morning when the Commissioner told me to go and hear an assault case from a place called Odumase. Very shy and very nervous I obeyed. Somehow or other the registrar or clerk or interpreter (he varies his title from time to time as circumstances demand) got me into my chair, and a prisoner was brought in. He certainly had been assaulted by someone. Then appeared the complainant, who also showed signs of manhandling. Prisoner pleaded guilty. Complainant said he was sitting in the street at Odumase with some friends. Prisoner came along, also with friends. Without any reason prisoner then assaulted him. Six witnesses confirmed this story.

Prisoner, when asked to explain, stated that it was quite true. He had hit the complainant, but the complainant had started the row. He, the prisoner, was coming down the street with his friends when suddenly complainant rushed out of his house and hit him. Witnesses were six of his friends.

In the end both parties were bound over. That was all. I came out of court and asked the interpreter what had happened. He said no one had been assaulted. The wounds in both cases were self-inflicted. The complainant had arrived first, and so defendant had got locked up for one night. There had been a palaver over a girl between the two men. The complainant hoped to jail his adversary, so he knocked himself about; defendant heard of this and did the same. But he was beaten into Sunyanî by a short head. Being arrested, he naturally pleaded guilty on the grounds that the white man always pays more attention to a guilty man!

This rather worried me; so at lunch I told the Provincial Commissioner. He laughed and gave me the sound advice never to worry over a decision once given. But my tale had aroused in him a reminiscent mood. It was then his last tour in West Africa, where he had been for eighteen years. He told me story after story, of which I remember only two.

"Once," he said, "just after the resettlement of Ashanti after the 1900 rebellion, a gang of men was going around the countryside 'money-doubling.' Their procedure was simple. On arriving at a village they gave out that they were emissaries of the bush-gods, who had sent them to help the villagers, and the gods would give them great wealth. They then proceeded to erect a temple, rather on the structural lines of a confessional. In the evening, when all was ready, one of the gang entered the temple to communicate with the gods. The others then announced that whosoever gave money to the gods would receive back twofold as a reward for their faith and trust. An accomplice made a deposit; and the one who was in the temple, taking it, said he would remit the money to the monkeys to carry to the bush-gods, and that on the morrow he knew the gods would return it twofold. A villager (why are villagers all the world over so credulous?) followed suit, succeeded by a second, and a third. Then the man said that the monkeys would have enough to do for one night.

"Next evening everyone repaired to the temple; and, sure enough, the money was returned twofold to those who the night before had trusted and believed in the gods' desire to help them. Then many came forward; and only when night fell did the gifts cease.

"The following morning the gang had disappeared. At once the villagers sent word to the Commissioner. They never warned the next village, where the swindle was again perpetrated.

"And so it went on, until at last the Commissioner got into touch with the gang and arrested the lot. But of six hundred pounds odd alleged to have been taken, only the sum of fifty pounds or so was found on them.

"Now, it was essential that justice should be done, and the money restored. The villagers pointed out that now they no longer had chiefs with power to help them; that the white man had promised to be their father and their mother; that they had not killed the thieves, as they would have done in the not-long-distant past, after learning where the money had been hidden, but had, very nobly, listened to the white man's promise and had forgone their lawful revenge.

"The prisoners made no excuses. They admitted that they had received the money, and had fulfilled their part of the bargain and given the money to the monkeys; that they did not doubt but that the monkeys would have brought back twice the amount from the bush-gods had it not been for the stupendous folly of the white man in interfering, and that now, of course, the gods would be most unlikely to return even the original loans.

"I was in a quandary," he said. "That money had to be recovered. So I bluffed. When they all agreed the money had gone to the monkeys, I ordered the sergeant to march out one of them and shoot him. He did so, and when the volley was over, a second was sent out. When there were only two left, I gave them a bit of time to talk it over; but they refused to say where the money was, except that it was with the monkeys. Then only one was left, and I said I would give him half-an-hour to think it over, but that before I shot him the soldiers would play with him for a while. He surrendered, and betrayed the hiding-place of the money. It took three days to fetch and have it checked. It had been buried at three different villages. The man himself went with me and an escort. On our return he met the other four, who, naturally, were uninjured.

"Highly illegal, my boy," he added, "but those were hard days. Incidentally, action like that is very dangerous. You never can tell whether these men will not die of fear or sheer cussedness."

The second case was not quite so grim. He was holding court when a terrible shindy occurred, and two women rushed in, pushing aside prisoner and ushers and police. They both began talking and shouting. But calm was restored, and it was explained that they disputed the ownership of a baby. Baby was produced and laid on the Commissioner's desk, all naked but happy.

" Ah," said the Commissioner, turning to his clerk. " Mr Kwami, I think we know this case. If you look up Solomon on civil law you will find the verdict."

Mr Kwami retired to the office, but returned saying that the Government had not supplied the court with Mr Solomon's work.

" No matter, I remember the decision," said the Commissioner. " Sergeant, is your bayonet sharp? No? Well, there is the butcher's knife. Cut the baby in half—no, not that way—that apparently tickles him—lengthwise; but let us first consider the claimants. Madam, do you agree to my cutting this baby in half? "

The baby by this time was on the Commissioner's knee, very happy with a watch-chain, and quite indifferent to its mothers.

" Certainly—as the white man wishes," replied number one.

" You are our father and our mother: certainly I agree to what you say," said number two.

" Mr Kwami, Solomon was not a wise man. Sergeant, keep the baby, and when it is hungry it will choose its own mother."

I pointed out that that could hardly settle it. He said no—nor could he; but in any case, as everyone, except himself, knew all the facts, no injury would happen to the baby. As a matter of fact the mother was dead, and the two women were aunts, and apparently took turn about with the baby.

There is no moral to that tale. It merely shows that procedure in our remoter courts is not quite as at home. An element of reality is here, and more often than not the cold formality of a court of justice is warmed and the atmosphere of a kindly children's court produced.

But Sunyanî was far from being a station where court cases were the most important part of one's life. Work was very varied; but there is no need to catalogue all that a Commissioner is supposed to do.

There were five of us in all: the Commissioner, the doctor, a soldier-man who soon left for the war, a public-works man, and myself. We had a weird habit of taking a Sunday walk to Odumase to view the cemetery. That seems a morbid occupation, but it provided a walk and ensured proper care being taken of our dead, for Odumase had been a station once, until it was found to be too unhealthy. As a matter of fact, in nearly all out-stations the cemetery is close to one—often within full view of one's front door. A curious idea that, until one remembers that we of a Northern race keep our dead close to us. Is not the village green more often than not close to the churchyard? Is not the churchyard or its surrounding wall the rendezvous of the youth until such time as they enter the public-house alongside? There is no irreverence in this. Our dead are part of ourselves, and we like them near us instead of in the lonely and remote cemetery of a town, where they lie, as it were, no longer a part of our lives, but almost as outcasts from our minds. I think that is why we do not make our cemeteries out here far away.

It is always the cemetery that strikes one first on approaching a station. Even at Sekondi—the day I first landed—we three new-comers, not fearful of the heat and desirous of seeing the place, went for a stroll along the cliffs, and the first thing we met with was the funeral of a white man ; and only the other day I noticed from the sea the white tombstones standing out as the most prominent feature in the landscape.

The road to Odumase was not in the forest. That ends in a long, more or less straight line of white tree-trunks at Sunyanî, when so-called orchard-bush is encountered. If the grass is young, one can see a resemblance to an overgrown, ill-kept and unkempt orchard, badly planted and never pruned. Otherwise the resemblance is a far-fetched one. The grass for the greater part of the year is over six feet high ; the trees are too close together or too large ; there are patches of the former forest. Farther north—and a considerable way north—the bush does begin, in a slight way, to resemble an orchard ; but here, I suppose, the first who saw it, after the monotony of the forest, were so delighted that they could think only of that delightful thing, an English orchard. Thus this type of " bush " acquired a misleading name.

But orchard-bush to a European has many advantages over the forest. One can get shooting there, which in the darkness of the trees is difficult ; one can see, and therefore one believes he inhales a purer air ; it is not so damp. These advantages are about equally balanced by disadvantages which I hope to make clear later. But here at Sunyanî the country alongside the Odumase road gave us shooting—bush-fowl and green pigeon in abundance, sometimes the guinea-fowl of the grassland, rock-partridge, and ocasionally smaller antelopes. Anyway, it gave us an excuse for an evening stroll with a gun.

One evening the Commissioner, the doctor and myself had returned from our weekly visit to Odumase, and we went over to the medical officer's for our pre-dinner drink, as it was his turn; we took it in turn to dispense evening hospitality. The Commissioner first walked over to his bungalow, and I went on with the doctor. Outside his house the chairs had been drawn out as usual, and George was waiting by mine with my coat. As he helped me on with it he said that a new white man had been in to see me.

There was nothing very unusual about this. Only a few days before a European had suddenly arrived, a merchant travelling rapidly on his cycle. So we asked where he was. He said that the man had entered the house, sat down for a while and read one of my magazines. He never spoke to the boy, and refused a whisky-and-soda, and had, after finishing his pipe, got up and without a work gone off in the direction of the town. He was a tall man with a black beard.

The only other European in the station at the time was the P.W.D. man, and he was neither tall nor had he a beard. But the war had just started, and a tally was being kept of any Europeans who might enter the district. So when the Commissioner came over I told him, and he said: "Oh! we must call him up, and put him up somewhere." He then wrote a note and enclosed it in another to one of the clerks, asking the latter to have it given to the European who had just arrived.

To our surprise the answer came back that no white man had arrived; that he, the clerk, had been all the afternoon and evening on his verandah and that no one had passed from any bungalow into the town. He suggested, however, that it was probably the ghost.

By this time the P.W.D. man had joined us, so I asked him if he had been over to see me. He said he had not, but that he had been out with a ·22 I had lent him, and on his return he had gone straight home, had had a bath, and had then come over to the doctor's. We told him of my visitor and the clerk's communication.

Unexpectedly he concurred in this, and informed us that his night-watchman had frequently seen the ghost, who was tall and black-bearded. Now the only European buried there was a young man, fair-haired and beardless, and certainly not tall. He had been well known to the night-watchman, who therefore would not have made any mistake.

We never learned the explanation of that mystery.

But the most amusing episode in my sojourn at Sunyan was Percy. He was a young chimpanzee, whose mothe had been killed by a local hunter. Percy was very angr over this and had attacked his mother's assassin, with th result that he was captured and brought in to Sunyan for sale.

I think five pounds was his purchase price, which th Commissioner paid. Percy then settled down and gre up a well-behaved youth. He was easy to train and ver quick to learn to imitate his master. He was naturally rather a nuisance, having to be left behind whenever the Commissioner went on tours of inspection in his province. Thus it came about that he was given to the G.C. Regiment stationed at Coomassie, where he became an honorary member of the mess.

But city life spoilt Percy. Either he had too many masters, or his too-gay life upset his balance. In any case he became somewhat obstreperous, and his popularity began to wane, until one day the limit was reached. Percy attacked a small child, and either bit off its hand, or scratched it, or frightened it; and that cost his brother officers half-a-crown for compensation—in threepenny-bits. The child's tears were dried up; and Percy was sentenced to exile, and sent back to Sunyanî, to the Commissioner, his master.

Although departing thus under a cloud, he was allowed to retain his honorary rank and membership of the mess, and so preserved to himself the great delight of uniform and mess kit, which Percy loved, and which he insisted on wearing on every possible occasion.

The disgraced chimpanzee arrived without mishap at Sunyanî, where the P.W.D. man took him in charge, and trained him almost as well as his more famous relative, Consul, who had had so great a furore in shows and on the stage in Europe. Percy learned to smoke pipes and cigarettes—he could extract a match from its box, light it and apply it to his smoke; he could ride a bicycle for a short distance, but he usually poised himself on the framework and spoilt everything by trying acrobatic feats; he could drink and eat in European fashion; he dressed and undressed himself; he was very popular with the children, whom he used to chase with a stick, but never hurt any of them, while they played "tag" with him; he was especially fond of the village carpenter, who never seemed to mind his coming, but always had a little snack waiting for him.

But he could not remain for ever in this happy state. He was certain to become dangerous as he grew older, so he was sold to Hagenbeck of Berlin.

Then came the war. Percy became a prisoner of war, and whether in obedience to the order to send all Germans back to Europe, or merely because chance had it so, Percy was ordered home. His P.W.D. master and trainer was returning for leave, and Percy would accompany him.

It was decided by the Commissioner and the soldier-man to give Percy a farewell dinner. That *was* a dinner. Percy of course came in full kit and joined in gins-and-bitters before the meal. No one knows how many he took, but he sat down quite sober and good. He took soup and fish and sherry. His fowl was carefully cut up for him and some yams and peas mashed up. A very little champagne in its proper glass—for Percy never, except in temper, broke a glass—was also given him.

And then Percy suddenly saw an open box of dried figs in front of him. This was more than he could stand. With a terrific war-cry he rose on his chair and stabbed the luscious fruit with his fork. He forgot all his manners, and as each forkful of figs disappeared into his pouches he gave another yell of triumph and greed. His master prepared to remove him. Percy saw the inevitable, drank his champagne, and pathetically went like a child from the table, to stand disgraced in a corner. However, he could not be left like that, as one never knows quite what a chimpanzee once aroused will do, for they are terribly strong; so he was taken home and put to bed.

Next day, Percy, very sorry for himself, went away. I last saw him in 1922 in our own Zoo. Poor Percy! From being a pet he had become an ignominious exhibit, and, saddest of all, was hopelessly twisted up with rheumatism. For a long time he had been kept in his own rooms and indulged in all his little fancies; but he grew too savage. He seemed to know anyone from West Africa and greeted me effusively, but his keeper was always fearful lest he should break out, which, one day, he did, and attacked a lady who was visiting him. So Percy left his private rooms and became a tenant of a public cage.

Soon after Percy had left I too went away from Sunyanî, to take over my first district, Asunafo-Ahafo.

CHAPTER IV

TO GOASO

ON my arrival at Sunyanî I had met the then Commissioner of Asunafo-Ahafo, who had come into provincial headquarters over some matters. It was his first tour too, and he had just finished his twelve months, most of which had been at Goaso. He had waxed enthusiastic over the place, and talked of little else.

I remembered, as I left Sunyanî, how he had told me that the route to Goaso through the forest was just like a tunnel, so thick was the overgrowth of the tree-tops. I was a little sceptical, but I soon found he was not far wrong, for in less than a quarter of an hour from Sunyanî one entered the forest, no longer a wide sun-bathed path, but a track in deepest shade, here and there speckled with light, strained as it were through holes in the leaf-made roof. No longer existed the riot of jungle on either side, bright greens and gorgeous flowers, but a carpet of rotting leaves, stuck, as a pincushion with pins, with dark-leafed plants, all leggy, in their endeavour to reach the rays of the sun; the tree-trunks stood up straight like countless telegraph-poles, but with their tops two hundred feet or so above, and their colour mostly dark green; and here and there rose a mighty white or grey giant, with enormous buttresses, which made veritable caverns with their parent trunk.

HOUSE BUILDING.
The men are carrying shaped bricks of dried mud, which are built in layers to a height of 5ft.

AT THE WATERING PLACE.
A typical scene in the Dagomba country.

FLAILING MILLET.
A common scene in the Dagomba country. All the family are helping.

It was beautifully cool, owing to the shade and the dampness of the ceaseless drip from the tree-tops, but scarcely a good place for one who suffered from rheumatism. Bird-life was not visible, albeit there must have been plenty, as one could hear their voices and frequently the creaking and flapping of the ungainly wings of the larger birds, such as the giant toucan. But insect-life there was in abundance. Everyone is familiar with this aspect of tropical forest life—the multitudinous and multicoloured insects. In a separate chapter I give some notes on observations which may be of interest.

That was a walk to remember. I was *en route* to my first command, and everything seemed to be on its best behaviour. It took five days' trekking to reach my goal, but in spite of fatigue they were five days of undiluted pleasure. I had a hammock with me, but I refused to ride at all, for I felt too much happiness in these novel surroundings to grow tired, and only when the day's march was over did my limbs begin to ache.

The first march brought me to a small village called Atroni. A swamp marked its entrance, but swollen with the rains it had become quite a large pond, reminding one of the Pool of Silence of Mr Stacpoole. Eight hours that march took, through dark shady forest, over a woodland path twisting and winding apparently aimlessly, with great roots and buttresses and fallen trees across it making it far from easy. I slept well that night in spite of cicadas, frogs and those screams of the tree-bear which made me believe that some wretched child was being cruelly sacrificed in some devilish fetish rites.

We made an early start—especially early—for that day

I was to cross into the Ahafo district, my future home. There was no mark to indicate the district boundary, as that had not been actually settled, but I knew that Atroni was the last village in the Sunyanî district, so when, after going a long way, I saw a path leading off to my left I knew I had reached my first village, a little settlement called Wahaminsu. It lay off the track, but I visited it, and took keener note, I think, of everything there was in the village than I have ever taken since. I mentioned this to the officer I was relieving and he told me he had done the same thing.

That night I slept at Ntortrorsu. The rest-house was a very pretty one, made of wood and thatched. The verandah was marked by a row of Norman arches, all in mud, erected in the first instance, till the mud dried, on a framework of split palm-stalks. This was an old form of Ashanti architecture, reminding one somewhat of the adobe houses in Mexico. In front of the house a pretty little garden had been laid out, and although scarcely six months old was already in appearance quite an old one, so rapid is the growth of plants and shrubs in this damp, torrid climate. The whole was set in a square cutting in the forest, the trees of which rose perpendicularly from one hundred and fifty to two hundred feet around one. It was just as if one were enclosed in a box.

Not far from Ntortrorsu on the Goaso road the path widened into one of the prettiest glades I have ever seen. Here the grass grew on either side—not the tall, rank grass usually met with, but short, bright green, almost meadow grass, all glistening with moisture and spangled with small bright blue and white and yellow flowers, with gaunt, grey-white, grotesque trunks of the forest giants as a background. I used to look forward to reaching that little glade whenever I passed that way, for it was a wonderful change from the usual dark dreariness of the real forest.

The last night of our journey I slept at Nkassaim—a pretty village, with a fine old man, Mensa, as its chief. This was only six miles from Goaso—two hours' marching. So early the next morning I hastened on to my future home.

Just before arriving at Goaso I reached the River Goa, where the people were already gathered to meet me. Two small boys paddled me across the stream in a hollowed-out tree-trunk, and, after greeting the assembled people, I climbed a steep cliff of bright red mud into the village itself.

The D.C. met me and took me up to the bungalow, where he dismissed the people. The house was quite a new one, but already had been surrounded with a delightful garden, in which, to my delight, were growing some fine roses and many beautifully striped crotons. The station was on a hilltop, but the view, at first novel, soon came to be quite dreary in its monotone of white trunks—legs, as it were, of a table clothed in a cloth of brown-and-green tree-tops.

The district was a new one. It had been created only some fifteen months before my arrival, and was merely started in an attempt to put an end to ceaseless trouble between the two divisions of the people, Mim and Kukuom, which on several occasions had led to bloodshed. The district was known as Asunafo-Ahafo, and in olden times had been the hunting and snail reserve for the Ashanti people of Coomassie. Some time in 1895 certain refugees from the capital had fled thither to escape execution at the hands of the Coomassie authorities. At that time the chief village was Mim, not far from which place was the famous sacred rock of Mim Mohan. The refugees were given sanctuary, and when the soldiers of Coomassie came to demand their surrender the people refused to give them up.

The soldiers returned, and on their report a small expedition was sent to enforce the demand and to exact punishment. When the Ahafo people heard this there was great consternation, and in a general meeting the decision to resist was come to, since punishment was certain in any case. But no man dared to take up the leadership of the revolt, until the chief of Kukuom, on a promise that he would be recognized by all as *Omanhene*, or master of the land, if victorious, agreed to command them. The chief of Mim was evidently playing a double game here, backing both sides, for he was undoubtedly at that time the most powerful chief in Ahafo; but he knew that if the rebels were vanquished their leader assuredly would, unless killed in battle, die horribly, and that if the revolt were successful his position as the chief of the majority of the people would most probably assure his eventual proclamation as *Omanhene*.

The Ahafos then withdrew into their forest, and the Coomassies came on, sure of victory over mere hunters and peasantry. But their cocksureness met with a terrible rebuff. The two forces came together near a village called Akrodi, and the royal troops were annihilated.

Victory, however, merely made matters worse for the rebels. The chief of Kukuom, now *Omanhene* of Ahafo, called all together, and on the advice of his sub-chiefs he decided that only by placing their country under British protection could they escape the vengeance of the Ashanti monarch. A deputation was sent in all haste, and was favourably received by the authorities. This treaty coincided with the downfall of Prempeh, the last ruler of Ashanti, so that as matters turned out Ahafo need never have revolted.

The chief of Mim thus had fallen between two stools, for the Government had recognized the chief of Kukuom as the *Omanhene*, in their treaty of protection, to which Mim had affixed his signature, thereby acquiescing in the implied suzerainty of Kukuom over Mim. He had never rested quietly under this rule. In the rebellion of Ashanti against the Government in 1900 Mim had again played a doubtful rôle, and afterwards, on two or three occasions, troops had had to be sent to patrol Ahafo. Affairs culminated in a very serious assault on one of Kukuom's principal court officials.

Every Ashanti chief has one or two men whom we call "linguists." These are his mouthpieces. They carry his messages for him, they alone can speak to him or repeat his words, for they are veritable ambassadors. One of these linguists had been sent to Mim. There he had been set on by some of the Mim people and made a prisoner. They had then most evilly tortured him by rubbing pepper (chillies) into the most tender parts of his body, and had it not been for the intercession of the chief of Nkassaim would have killed him. This chief, although a Mim subject, rescued the unfortunate fellow and sent him back to Kukuom.

Both sides armed; but a patrol arrived in time to prevent a fight, and it was decided to open a station in the district. The site chosen was at Goaso, a Mim village, almost exactly half-way between the two disputants; and as a further precautionary measure the people were made to construct a wide, ditched road—to-day we call them motor-roads, by which usually is meant a road, in favourable weather conditions, capable of being used by light cars—from Mim to Goaso, and from Goaso to Kukuom.

The day after my arrival at Goaso the D.C. had all the chiefs in to meet me, and then handed over the district. That evening we strolled through the village, which consisted of a lower and an upper town, and was in process of being removed to a better site, where my predecessor had marked out streets and avenues and town plots. I saw Kojo playing in the road and the departing D.C. arranged on my behalf with his mother that he should enter my household. He served me as faithfully as man can serve, and died in harness, more friend than servant.

Next morning the D.C. man departed and I began the first of many long periods alone in the bush, for my nearest white man was four days' distance away. There was never at Goaso very much work to do, and I had time to study an interesting paragraph issued on appointment by the Colonial Office indicative of the labours a Commissioner is expected to perform. This is the catalogue:

"The duties of an administrative officer are of a very varied character. He is the immediate agent of the Government in his district and his responsibility extends to all departments of the Administration which have not a special representative of their own at his station. Thus, in addition to his primary functions (*a*) of magistrate, and (*b*) of political officer (*i.e.* the officer responsible for the maintenance of satisfactory relations between the natives and the central administration), he may be called upon to take charge of a detachment of police; to perform the duties of accountant for his district; to superintend the district prisons; to supervise road construction, the clearing of waterways, or other public works. . . . Every officer is expected to do a certain amount of travelling, in the course of which he inspects the outlying portions of his district, transacts any necessary business with native chiefs, settles disputes between individuals or communities, and generally deals with all matters requiring the personal attention of a representative of the Government on the spot."

It seemed all-embracing enough, but later I learned one had to be half a veterinary, more or less able to render first aid, and to be something of a botanist and forestry man. But there is one duty euphemistically expressed in the list—that is, "to supervise other public works." This means, I have learned, that one must be a map-maker, a builder of bridges, an architect and a transport officer. It is evident that we Commissioners must be wonderful men. But since all this is expected of one, everything one does is taken for granted, and we usually hear: "That bridge of yours is a rotten one, d——d dangerous too." "Why ever did you build such a vile house? It not only leaks but it stifles one." "Thanks for the map, but you can't find your way with it." "Why ever didn't you tell me you had measles in the district?" "Man, man, don't you know anthrax when you see it?" "How many baobabs are there in your country? What? Never counted them? What do you do with your time?" etc., etc.

At Goaso there was not much work for one in one's magisterial capacity. There were a few simple claims for payment of debts, a few appeals from the chiefs' courts in connexion with damages in adultery cases, and very occasionally a criminal case. Prisoners were, therefore, very rare, and when one did succeed in getting one it would only be for a short while, for some petty assault or other trivial offence. But one day there was a murder.

I had just finished my breakfast and was idling on the verandah when I saw a procession of people approaching. It was apparent that something of importance was the matter. There was the chief of Kukuom himself under his state canopy—a gorgeous affair of many colours, umbrella-shaped—a crowd with him and two men carrying a load of something slung on a pole and all wrapped in a dirty native cloth. My interpreter accompanied them.

When they had come up to the door, and after I had greeted the chief, I asked what was the matter, and the interpreter said: "Big palaver." Then at a sign the bearers of the load put it down, unwound the cloth and disclosed the horribly mangled body of a girl-child.

The *Omanhene* then spoke to his linguist, who nodded and began to tell me the story. He ordered some men whom I had not observed particularly to step forward, two great big fellows, holding between them a little naked boy of about nine or ten years. This boy, the linguist told me, was the murderer. There had been a funeral custom the previous day at Kukuom, and as was usual the villagers were fasting. Now the dead girl and the boy were both of the *Omanhene's* household, and they also had not eaten that day. The boy became very hungry, and had importuned one of the women of the house until she had given him two plantains. While he was eating these, two little girls—one of whom was the deceased—came along, and seeing the boy eating begged also for food. The woman having nothing else at hand gave them a stalk of sugar-cane to chew, and went away. It appeared that the boy had seen this and wanted a piece of the cane. The girls refused, and the boy threatened to kill them unless they complied; but they laughed and said he was not a man. The boy then said they would soon see, and he went into one of the huts in the *Omanhene's* compound and came out with a flint-lock gun.

The gun was produced. It was much larger than the boy.

The girls then said that he did not know how to fire, and that they were not afraid. But he replied that he did know, and unless they gave him a piece of the cane they would soon see that he spoke the truth. However, they still refused, and the boy, fetching a powder-horn, knocked out a little on to the touch-hole. The two girls then became somewhat afraid and ran into the sleeping-hut of the *Omanhene*. The boy followed and again demanded some cane. The girls jumped up on to the chief's bed, and on their refusal the boy fired the gun. The result was before my eyes.

Now this put me in a quandary. The boy was quite possibly even less than nine years. No native could tell me. I had nowhere to put the child, for one could not place him in the common prison—a great airy but dark room—as he would have been there alone, for I had no prisoners at the time. His real parents did not live in my district.

I suggested that the chief should look after him. To this he demurred most vehemently. For not only was the child a murderer, but had he not actually violated the sanctity of the chief's couch? All he wanted me to do was to kill the boy.

I gave the child to my corporal of police and told the people to bury the little girl and return in three days. All this time the boy had not spoken a word, and was in a very bad state of terror.

As soon as the people had gone the corporal agreed to look after the boy if he could be guaranteed immune from punishment in the event of the child's escape or suicide. I then told the boy not to be afraid, and he was taken away. All that day and the next he refused to open his mouth, but on the third day the corporal told me he had told him all about it, and might be sufficiently reassured to tell me. I went over to see him, and after a few words quite irrelevant to the crime asked him for his version.

He then told me that it was quite true what everyone had said; he had killed the girl, but he did not mean to do that. He thought the gun he took was not loaded. He had been out the preceding day with its owner shooting squirrels (some are quite large animals), and on their return the gun had been unloaded and cleaned; therefore when he took the gun he intended only to frighten the girls, and he wanted to make a flash to make sure.

Next day I held the inquiry, the boy not being present, and all that part of his story about the squirrels and the cleaning was found true. The owner, however, had come back on the morning of the crime and had loaded his gun—for so he usually kept it. I then told the chief that I would send the boy to the Provincial Commissioner, who would deal with the case. Needless to say, the wretched boy was given back to the care of his real parents, who were warned not to send him again to Kukuom.

I have said that one was not overbusy at Goaso. By that I meant that the office work was far from burdensome, for as a matter of fact then, as to-day, the one trouble in a Commissioner's life is that he cannot do all that the natives want him to do for them, in their intense keenness to progress.

I have lived in the Western States, and in Western Canada have seen town sites erected out of the forest, and thriving townships grow up, quicker than the proverbial mushroom. I have quite a close acquaintanceship with Western real estate offices and Western newspapers; and once was quite prepared to prove that Hunger Harbour or Cardinallsville were undoubtedly destined to become the centre of the industrial, financial and agricultural world; moreover, I could draw maps showing the future convergence thither of every imaginable railway or steamship line. That was publicity, advertisement or, euphemistically, optimism, in which few probably concurred.

One did not expect to find the same spirit in the Ashanti bush. However, one did; and that same anxiety to go ahead, to progress, is still as rampant as ever. Here in Goaso, wherever one might go, there were always demands for motor-roads. Unfortunately one does not have the time. Work such as that required personal supervision and was naturally very slow. Finishing Goaso station, erecting rest-houses at most of the villages, laying out a large town site at Mim, another at Kukuom, and aligning the new houses at Goaso, making a motorable road towards Coomassie, and travelling over the district, kept one on the move if not at work at full pressure.

It was the travelling that appealed most to me, however interesting the making of roads and bridges or the laying-out of town sites; and the more one travels in one's district the more, of course, one learns. What is more attractive even than that is that one gets into closer touch with the people. It is far easier to call at a man's house in the less-frequented parts and have a short conversation with him on farming and weather (not only in England is weather discussed) than it is to call on one's next-door neighbour. The former is pleased, natural and open; the latter may be pleased, but he won't be natural, for he realizes too well one's position; and he will be secretive, wondering why he should be selected for a visit, and worried as to what sanitary law his household may have broken.

There was plenty of opportunity for travelling at Goaso, owing to the newness of its creation as a district and to the fact that both of my predecessors had been fully occupied with building the station and making the road from Mim to Kukuom. I did not hesitate to avail myself of the chance, and was nearly always about in the district.

The best trek I ever did was a long one into country partly unvisited and partly only once before visited. This was towards the area bordering on the Bia river, which was my western boundary. The map of that part was a simple one to read: it was just a spotless white mark; but there was no difficulty in reaching the Bia, as every villager was acquainted with one or other of the routes, for there were many, since this was the great snail-collecting country of Ashanti.

CHAPTER V

TREKKING THROUGH FOREST & JUNGLE

SNAILS are one of the most important articles of food among the forest people. I do not think any estimate has ever been made of the value of the trade in them, but it must be quite colossal. In the district of Ahafo lies one of the most valuable areas for catching snails in the country, and the natives have apparently learnt a lot about their natural history. In 1924, for instance, the old men and chiefs in Ahafo agreed to forbid snail-catching for three years, as they were beginning to fear the possibility of the complete destruction of the stock.

The proper season for collecting the snails is at the beginning of the rains, and lasts for about six weeks. Whole villages—men, women and children—migrate into the forest, leaving only the old and infirm to look after their homes. Arrived on the hunting-ground the people erect temporary shelters with sticks and leaves, make settees from branches—on which they will sleep—and generally prepare for quite a holiday.

Everyone goes out each morning, returning quite late in the evening. The snails are found crawling over the moistened leaf-carpet of the forest and often climbing up the trees. They are rather more like cockles than our own snails, and some run to immense sizes. But these are not much liked, as they are too tough. It is rather a funny sight to see a naked youth with a basket on his head full of live snails—crawling over each other, down the boy's back, all over him. He brings his load back to the camping-place, empties the basket on a great heap, and off once more he goes to the chase.

Meanwhile, near the great heaps of snails, women are at work. One sits close to the pile, having in her hands two wooden mashers—very much alike to the butter-patters at home. She takes a snail, smashes up its shell and drops the pulped mass in front of her. Extreme skill is used in this at times, for one will notice some women so deft at the work that they actually separate the shell from the snail while patting it. Opposite this woman sits another, who picks up the smashed snail and impales it on a wooden skewer, of which she has a number in front of her. She makes a careful selection of the snails in order to grade them. There are a hundred snails on each skewer, and twenty skewers are made into a bundle. Two such bundles make a load of the average weight carried by these people—approximately sixty pounds.

When a skewer is full it is set in front of a fire, the snail-meat being then dried. Afterwards it is smoked *en masse* on elevated grids.

The value of this trade to the Ahafo people must be very great. A skewer varies from ninepence to one shilling and ninepence, so that with an average price of one shilling one will get forty shillings for a load. It may seem extraordinary that one could get snails in such quantities. But once one has learned to detect them among the leaves, one will soon perceive thousands. They seem to dwell in colonies or patches. After the heavy rains one rarely meets with them, and I do not know where they go to.

This snail-hunting is regulated by the chiefs and elders, who fix the time for the people to go out into the forest, give permission for strangers to collect on payment of a tithe—one skewer in ten—agree on the area to be collected on and decide questions of village boundaries in the forest. But it is to a European an unpleasant business. The smell is horrid; and snails at the best of times are not really jolly companions. Eating them, however, must be worse, for they become a trifle high after the smoking. I am told they are quite nice, but very mucilaginous. The story is told of a European who had some once in the usual native form, in soup. He bit a piece of the snail-meat—but he had false teeth . . .

The route I followed to the Bia was along the Ashanti boundary of the Gold Coast. Nothing of particular interest occurred until we drew near to Aboom, where the people, warned of my intentions, had built me a palm-leaf camp in a beautiful site. They had selected a little eminence just off the path, which was quite treeless. On one side was a precipice, giving a really fine view of forest-clad hills, all tinted and multicoloured, reminding one of autumn shades in England. To my surprise I could make out what were evidently some European bungalows. These I learned were the deserted dwelling-places of Europeans who had once endeavoured to open

IN THE KONKOMBA BUSH.
A typical hut of a Konkamba farmer, made of sun-dried mud, with grass roof. The blades of grass jutting out enable the rain to fall clear of the walls.

GROUP OF KONKOMBA.
A group of men returning from their farms. The shyness of several is very noticeable.

up this part for mining. Transport troubles killed their venture.

A chief from the colony, accompanied by his people, came in to visit me. He and his courtiers were richly bedecked in gold ornaments, all of native workmanship, and therefore grotesque and crude in their designs. I returned his visit that afternoon. The path was a very hilly one and remarkable for an almost continuous series of deep round holes, like embryo wells, which lay on either side of the road. These were the old native gold-workings, long since abandoned. But more striking to see was the number of snakes which basked in the sun on the hillsides—black ones, green ones, grey ones, large and small, thick and thin—there must have been over a hundred in the mile-and-a-half stretch of path.

I have heard that snakes are not common in this country. This is very far from being the case, but it requires a trained eyesight to discern a motionless snake, just as much as it does to see wild animals in their own pastures. The annual death-roll due to snake-bites has never been taken, but from my own experience, and that of immediate acquaintances, I presume it is not less than in India. To give an idea of the number of snakes in the country it suffices, I think, to record that the German zoological authorities identified seventy-five different species in southern Togoland alone!

From Aboom I proceeded to a very small village called Saesu. For the first time in my life I saw stark naked men at work at this place. They ran away on viewing me, but after a while returned and became, as is the rule, quite friendly and extremely hospitable.

The next day provided a very long march through magnificent forest, where one was almost always in the shade and where one could obtain quite a long view. It took seven hours to reach Pomakrum, or the village of Poma. On the way I stopped on hearing an extraordinary din—quite indescribable, for at times it was a roar, at times a squeal. I waited for Kojo to come up and explain. This he did by going off into the bush and returning in a moment or two with a gigantic beetle, marked in black-and-white. This was a specimen of the so-called Winnebah beetle, the largest coleopter in the world, I believe.

Poma was a woman-chief. She came down the path to greet me dressed in a magnificent native cloth of many colours, of silk and cotton and gold thread, a gorgeous patchwork. She was accompanied by only two men, but by a crowd of girls and women. On viewing me they all gave tongue to a terrible din, resembling a Tyrolese yodel without the final chord; and after the customary handshake the old lady—for Poma was a very old woman—danced in front of me all the way to her village—to me a very embarrassing performance.

The village was like one of those described by former visitors to Ashanti, of a type now almost unknown. There was no main street. All the huts were massed together, with only the narrowest of passages between. Completely round the village was a cleared space, serving as the principal meeting-place, scrupulously clean and studded with great shade-giving trees. Hither I was accompanied by the singing, dancing crowd, and conducted to a hut right in the very centre of the village, which had been made ready for me.

Ashanti huts of the old pattern had no rooms. They consisted usually of four or more shelters raised on mud plinths, which were kept scrupulously clean and shiny by constant renewal of a red wash. All these shelters were enclosed on only three sides, the fourth opening on to a yard. There was no possible privacy, as I found to my embarrassment when I took a bath.

That evening Poma told me how her village had come to arise. She had accompanied an Ashanti expedition against some of the Ivory Coast tribes, and on their return had obtained leave to settle on the Bia. It obviously was good hunting country, both for meat and snails, and the river afforded the opportunity of plenty of fishing. One companion, a female, remained with Poma; and some young men had cleared a little farmland and had built a hut for them, before leaving the two behind.

Poma's real reason for stopping I could not learn. However, she was determined to found a village, and with this in view made the rule that no man should marry either of them or any other girl who might join them; that men could stop only a while in the village, and would have no rights at all over any children born as a result of the inevitable intercourse between them and the village women. It might seem that two defenceless women alone in the forest would have been carried off by the first man who came along, but in Ashanti there is a greater protection than strength of arm can afford—that is, the defence which the careful use of witchcraft and magic and credulity will give. Her scheme succeeded, and I believe there were some two hundred inhabitants in the village when I visited it.

The old chieftainess produced for my perusal a strip of paper on which words were written in 1901 to the effect that Poma had been loyal throughout the rising of 1900. The paper was signed by the one and only Englishman who had ever visited the village up till then, which is easy to understand because of its very remoteness. But her pleasure and pride in its possession persuaded me to give the old lady another.

An interesting little incident occurred at Pomakrum. Kojo opened for me a tin of biscuits manufactured by a well-known firm at Carlisle. Inside the airtight-tin wrapper was a note written in a childish hand by a girl, who presumably had packed the tin, asking the discoverer of her note to write to her—she gave the address—in Carlisle and let her know where the tin was opened. Naturally I complied with the request, and wondered if she would ever locate Pomakrum.

After visiting the confluence of the two rivers, Saesu and Bia, I pursued my way upstream. It was very difficult marching. The path was wide enough, but it was no longer forest country, it was pure jungle. The road was actually a tunnel through brambles and thorn-bushes, and it was so dark, although the sun was well up, that one could not read a book of fairly large print. I tried. The great difficulty, however, was that the carriers could not stand upright with their loads, and miserably had to proceed all stooping and bent. Tracks of small antelope were common, and several buffalo had also been about. We saw none, however.

On the second day upstream from Pomakrum a village on the right bank, which was in the colony, heard of my arrival, and sent me, as a present, a dead leopard, which had been killed on the morning of my coming. It was a magnificent specimen, small, but with an extra-yellow shade to its extra-long fur. This animal had been killed by a hunter who had called it to him. Elsewhere in these pages I have endeavoured to describe that truly remarkable form of hunting.

Eventually I reached a very small village called Domeabra. Here the chief of Mim had promised to send me a guide, as we had to leave the river and trek across the forest, following, if possible, the trails of hunters and snail-collectors. But no guide was there. However, a youth of the village said he could find the way, but that it was a long road, and he doubted if I could do it in one day.

That trek was the longest day's march I have ever done or ever hope to do. We started at five-thirty A.M. in a cold mist, due to the dry season with its northerly wind, which caused near the river most rapid evaporation. The path was very hard to see, and eventually petered out into footprints with a dwarf tree-like plant of a deep olive-colour growing between each step. It was easier to lope along than walk.

I hurried on, and to my great anxiety saw nowhere any traces of water. We passed the track of a large solitary elephant—the first I had ever seen—but did not wait. I rested for an hour at one P.M. and resumed the march. The carriers were far behind, but my cook and Kojo had passed me. At ten P.M. I was practically all in, when we heard the sound of drumming in the distance. In a short time people appeared with lamps and guided me into a village. I was so tired that I was almost unable to keep my balance on a tree-trunk which acted as a bridge over a stream at the village entrance—the first water we had met with that day. The village was Mim Mohan.

It was particularly to avoid this village that I had asked the chief of Mim to send a guide, for orders had been issued not to go there unless absolutely necessary, as there was no point in upsetting the religious susceptibilities of the people, for Mim Mohan was the village specially dedicated to the spirit which dwelt in the great rock near by, which was visible from one end of the street, a fairly lofty mass of grey granite.

The spirit was said to be the son of the spirit of the holy River Tano, and had revealed himself in a way reminiscent of Jewish history; for it was the tradition that a certain hunter had been lost in the forest here, and he came to this rock. There he rested, and, almost dying of hunger, had prayed to his ancestors and his gods for help. To his surprise, the next day, and every day for seven years, food was brought to him by vultures. The god evidently revealed himself to the man, for he learned many languages and acquired much magic, and eventually found the way back to his people. His reception was far from cordial, but by his magic he overcame their terror, and led them to the dwelling-place of the spirit which had helped him.

Travellers from afar came to hear of this wondrous place, and the inhabitants grew wealthy and more numerous. Mim was then founded. There are restrictions without number involved in the worship of this spirit, and when I departed the chief of Mim had to sacrifice eight sheep to cleanse the place: two because a white man had been there, one because my clerk had worn boots, two because my carriers had spat on the ground, one because I had smoked tobacco, one because we had violated the sanctity of the place by not sacrificing before our entry, and the eighth, so far as I could learn, in case we had done some other evil thing which had not been noticed.

The next day was a very short trek into Mim, the largest town in the district and one of the largest purely Ashanti towns in the country. The route was a remarkable one. It led along a wide lawn-like avenue, the grass being very short and most tidily kept; on either side at frequent intervals were wide offshoots, clear of grass and well swept, each leading to a stone set beneath a tree on which had been sacrificed a fowl or to which had been offered eggs or other food. This avenue, after about three-quarters of a mile, ended abruptly with a fallen giant of the forest, beyond which was apparently impenetrable jungle. Then for the first time I saw a native secret path. One climbed on to the trunk and carefully moving out of the way briers and creepers, which, after we passed, were replaced, one reached a small hollow in the jungle, into which one descended. There seemed to be no exit, but our guide from the sacred village soon showed me how all the bramble and other impedimenta could be lifted up and replaced. Thus one could pass, and leave no trace that there was any path save for the absent dewdrops shaken by our passage. This turned and twisted for about a hundred yards, and led us on to the main path from Mim to Wam and the hinterland.

I had occasion at a later date to see just such another path. The Mim and Kukuom troubles again came to a head, and the Mim people actually cut paths parallel to the roads leading to the station and Goaso in order to waylay the chief of Kukuom and his people. My corporal of police, an Ashanti, took me, when we had averted the trouble, to see them, and we found guns and powder secreted along them. It was really a very fine piece of woodmanship; I could see nothing but a tangled mass of jungle, yet one could pass along the path without being caught by any brier or tripped by any creeper.

After my return from the Bia river I stayed some time at Goaso, busy with the marking of sites and streets, etc., in the new township. Life was rather lonely, but always interesting. There were incidents of all sorts to vary the monotony. I once adjourned the Court to go and shoot a large serval cat which had been robbing my hen-roost. The animal came across a lawn and went under a large tree that had recently been felled. Everyone enjoyed the hunt that ensued. Another morning I listened to what seemed a pack of hounds giving tongue. I asked Kojo what animals made that noise. He at once became frightened and told me not to look, because the noise came from some birds, to see which was death. I never fathomed this.

Then there was the garden, and insects, and wild

flowers. In the evening, if I was tired of reading, Kojo and Kobina came and told me fairy tales, or amused me with the game of cat's cradle. I wish I had taken notes. The game is played as at home, with a piece of string tied together so as to make an endless length. Each pattern has a name, and the two children would agree on one to start with. For instance the pattern known as "Palm-tree" would be taken. Both children would make this with their string, then one would call another, "Parrot," and the second child having made this would reply with a third, "Dog," and so on until one of the players was stumped. I once saw Kojo go as far as thirty-eight, by which time he was using his toes as well as his hands and neck!

It was the custom to bring me, either for sale or as a present (which is more expensive, for one has to give a present of a higher value in return), or just simply to show me, anything which arrived out of the ordinary. One could have procured quite a menagerie in this way. Two or three baby monkeys, a couple of civet cats, or rather kittens, a fine little black-and-white cat of I knew not what species, a harnessed antelope, a small blue duiker, and a leopard cub were all thus brought to me. I refused all save one civet cat, which eventually I freed. One cannot keep pets unless one can stay with them, and travelling one's district—if done properly—does not leave much time for home-life. The leopard cub was most fascinating. It was brought me by a wild-looking man, naked save for innumerable charms hanging from his neck, round his loins, on his knees and arms and ankles and wrists. He explained that he had come across the mother leopard playing with her cubs. She had three of them, and having apparently winded him she took away one in her mouth. He did not know where her lair was, but waited till she returned for a second cub, and as this took some time he knew it was not too near. As soon as she had lifted it and gone off, the hunter seized the third and made for Goaso.

I took the cub from him. It was a really nice pet, all black, with tabby-coloured marks. But when I began to fondle it, it tore my arm badly, and that, together with the price asked, five pounds, made me decline the offer. The man returned to the village, but was not allowed to remain there that night, as the people were afraid the mother leopard would follow her offspring. The man, however, escaped this danger and sold the cub to a European in the colony. He was a curious man, and I should have liked to have learned more about him. The people told me that he was not a proper man at all, he was a witch; and that there were several like him, who lived alone without a hut in the forest, supporting life on snails and fruit and roots. I wonder what exactly was meant—whether he was a madman, an outlaw, or one of the survivors of the forest people whom the Ashanti had replaced.

One afternoon I saw a band of men approaching the bungalow. Eight of them were carrying a long shapeless mass, which they deposited some distance away in an uncleared patch of rough land, where the forest had been cut down but the ground had not yet been brought into the lawned confines of the station. One of them came across to me and explained they had brought a big thing for me to see. I went, and saw a huge python. It had had its head cut off, also the tip of its tail; but it was still writhing and twisting about. They told me that it had been killed more than two hours previously, and related how a Moshi labourer, hired by one of the villagers to work on his farm, had noticed the snake lying coiled about a branch of a fallen tree. The brute was asleep, and the man had first cut some skewers of a strong wood and had thrust these into the body. The snake roused, and showed its head, which the Moshi had at once cut off with his machete. This he carried back to the village, and other men had accompanied him to the scene. They had waited for the python to grow more or less quiet and had then carried it to me, first cutting off the tail, so as to avert any evil the snake might magically work. It was skinned for me and the men ate the meat. Minus the head and tail it measured twenty-one feet nine inches.

Goaso always seemed to provide something novel. My boys were ever a study full of surprises, but nothing was quite so startling as the treatment meted out to Kobina by his mother. He had been complaining about his head, so I sent for the woman. She told me it was nothing, and she would soon cure him. I next saw her pounding upon a stone a small quantity of green chilli peppers. When these were quite mashed into a paste she called Kobina, and holding him between her legs she put some of the mess into one of his eyes. He screamed and broke loose, pirouetting like one possessed. The woman quietly seized him and put some more into the other eye. She then calmly picked up the stones she had been using and remarked that the boy would soon be all right. He had meantime fled screaming into the bush. When he returned some time later he told me his headache was cured. I did not ask him how his eyes were.

One day a Forestry man came on a visit. He was very anxious to shoot some green pigeon that evening, so I pointed out a tree where they were feeding and he went off with a man to beat the birds out. He had not been long away when he came back and said: "No shooting for me. I am leaving the day after to-morrow. I would go to-morrow, but I must do some writing."

Naturally I wanted to know what was the matter, and he answered: "Flies!" just "Flies"—that was all.

Goaso district was a terrible place for flies; there were two varieties of tsetse, great big mango flies, large green ones, a nasty little one with black-and-white wings, and a drab-coloured one. There is no need to give their scientific names. They were "flies," and by "flies" in West Africa one always means biting flies, brutes that seemed to be crazed for love of human blood. Apparently they were too numerous to allow him to shoot.

It is impossible to exaggerate the fly pest as it obtains in Ahafo. Although people at home cannot believe the following, yet I must assure my readers of the truth of these happenings.

Apparently flies emerge *en masse* at certain seasons. Once I was walking along the road from Nkassaim to Goaso when I noticed on the back of a carrier walking in front of me a veritable swarm of insects. Suddenly, before I could say anything to the man, they left his back and came on me. Neck, face, arms and knees were attacked. The biting was so fierce that I could not find time, or rather had not sufficient endurance to free my hands from the task of beating them off and slapping my exposed members, to get my pipe and tobacco from my hip pocket. My boys ran up with my hammock, and I rolled myself into it and covered my knees with my coat while they rushed off with me out of the zone.

On another occasion I had sent my clerk, a native of course, down the motorable road towards Mim, where he was to deliver a note and bring back the answer, for which there was a hurry. He set out on his bicycle. He came back in less than an hour and told me he could not go on as the flies were too bad, but he would go after dark.

And lastly, Kojo remarked while he and I were running through one of these zones of flies in the Krachi district of Togoland—walking was impossible—that just before he had left Goaso to rejoin me on my return from leave the flies had been so bad for about a fortnight that no one had gone out on the roads at all except at night.

It is not always the same species that swarms like this, nor have I ever made notes of the dates on which they appear, though it is invariably during the rains, and usually just before a downfall.

In due time I bade Goaso farewell, leaving many real friends there and retaining the memory of many very happy days. I went direct to Coomassie, past the elephant-grass patches on the River Tano's banks, where in February, when the old grass has all been burnt and the new blades are but showing, the lordly bongo is to be seen in quantities, according to native report, and across the Tano itself, one of the great sacred rivers of Ashanti. For in its bosom resides the great spirit, sent from God, reverenced and worshipped by many thousands of the Twi-speaking people.

CHAPTER VI

FROM COOMASSIE TO TOGOLAND

I LEFT the forest with regret. That was only natural, for therein had been my first command. But, like most others, I always longed to go farther and farther inland, and when, after six months of purely magisterial work in the colony, I received orders to proceed to the Northern Territories, my excitement was great.

The Northern Territories consist of a tract of country to the north of Ashanti, reaching as far as the eleventh parallel of latitude. They form a protectorate of the Crown, and are made up of a portion of the great Dagomba-Moshi confederation and part of a Mandingo realm, which at the time of our advent on the scene was in a state of almost complete disruption. This was in 1897. To-day it is difficult indeed to visualize conditions as they obtained at that time. Unfortunately there is no record, save cold official documents, of what British officers found and saw there. Several still survive of that small band who took over the protection of the country. Perhaps one day one of them will record the story. It ill becomes me to attempt the picture.

But I think a summary of the conditions of the country is necessary for the understanding of that land. Imagine, therefore, a great area of grasslands, undulating but almost imperceptibly so, with numerous short (compared with the forest examples) trees, traversed by three great rivers from north to south and bounded on the south by a great waterway from west to east. There are no mountains; here and there is a hill, but of no striking prominence. As one gets farther north the trees become less in number; thorn-bush appears and tracts barren of grass—the first incursions of the desert, which lies still two hundred miles to the north.

The area of the Protectorate is small compared to the vastness of Africa. It is about forty thousand square miles, and unfortunately does not comprise the whole of any single nation. Force of circumstances and indifference on the part of the natives, because of incomprehension of our motives, caused the Great Powers to divide this portion of the world quite arbitrarily, and tribes have seen themselves cut in half, and parcelled out between France, Germany and ourselves.

There is no need to review here the history of the partition of Africa, nor trace the steps by which we took up the Protectorate, but one must recall that it is from this area and its surrounding country that the vast bulk of negroes were drawn for the slave traffic, which scarcely a quarter of a century ago was still thriving. It was here that the warriors of Samory and Babatu devastated the countryside in the last decade of the nineteenth century. Their imprint is still visible, for north of the forest zone the jungle does not soon return to wipe out man's passage.

When first we entered this Protectorate the Mandingo kingdom of the Gonjas was in a state of complete chaos as a result of prolonged civil war: the great confederation of the Dagomba was being divided up by the three contesting Powers—England, France and Germany: the western side was under the sway of Samory's hordes, the north-west was ravaged by Babatu, and the north-east, through our rival claims, was equally reduced to anarchy.

Then came the final delimitation between the Powers; Samory had been routed and captured by the French, and Babatu had been driven into a neutral zone—to Yendi. This zone was a great square containing Salaga and Yendi. It was eventually divided, the River Kulukpene or Daka being used as the Anglo-German boundary.

In 1907 matters had become more or less settled and a Civil Administration established.

Thither I was bound in 1916. The trek was more interesting than my fondest hopes had ever imagined. Coomassie, the railhead, was, and is still, the starting-off point for the traveller to the north. Twenty-five years ago one had to walk from Cape Coast to the eleventh parallel—about five hundred and fifty miles; fifteen years ago one trained to Coomassie and walked the remaining four hundred miles; five years ago one trained to Coomassie, motored to Ejura, and walked the balance of three hundred and forty miles; to-day one trains to Coomassie and can motor, during most of the year, as far as the eleventh parallel, our frontier with the French, and, if so inclined, could prolong the motoring many miles throughout the French Sudan.

I motored as far as Ejura. This is a drive really worth doing. The road was, and is, excellent, and never does it lack interest, nor is it rendered unpleasant by heat or sun.

One leaves the Coomassie rest-house as early as possible. This cannot be much before seven o'clock, because the loading of one's lorries is not a rapid piece of work. Countless, seemingly, are one's packages. There are cases of provisions for at least a twelvemonth; cases of drinkables; cases of all sorts of equipment; probably a crate for a bicycle; ammunition, guns; possibly a tent.

But it all gets stowed away whilst one is having an early breakfast, and then one's boys discover they are hungry! At last one starts, and the cars rattle and thunder through the streets of Coomassie.

Coomassie itself is not remarkable. The buildings are neither pretentious nor attractive. The plans on which they are constructed are, to say the least of it, simple. Imagine a row of oblong buildings, white-coloured, with a black dado about three feet deep. They all have a cheap-looking verandah, against the supports of which are leaning a few early native traders. Above their heads hang lines of Manchester cotton-goods, of every imaginable hue and pattern, on the floor are piled enamel basins and pots, bowls and pans of brass; if the shutters have been drawn one will see in the windows trays with every kind of trinket, masses of beads, scents, powders, etc.

But the streets are of interest. The cheap tawdriness of the buildings, all roofed with that vilest of civilization's products, corrugated iron (I live in a house roofed with it, so I am at least in a position to judge), flanks them. They run clean and straight and red-coloured, bearing masses of various-coloured people, all apparently enjoying the greatest happiness and all busy. There are not many loungers in the streets of Coomassie.

Five minutes and one is out of Coomassie, past a great cemetery, on to the Great North Road. What a road that is! For construction it might well be a high road in England; but for traffic it must be well-nigh unique. This road, used by a vast crowd of all conditions of men, leads to Timbuktu, the desert, and to unknown mysteries of Africa. There is none quite like it in all the world.

Just take a glance along this road for a few miles only from Coomassie. Here comes a group of Ashanti women, young girls, all laughing and merry, baskets of plantains and yams on their heads, bare of breast and with gaudy Manchester cloths around their waists and hips; here a band of tall, stately Moshi women clothed in white and with those attractive Biblical head-coverings hanging down their backs; there a small detachment of British soldiers, swarthy of mien, but proud in the uniform of his Majesty, neat and brisk, returning from some escort of specie to a remote station; here are forty to fifty men from the north beginning the weary thousand-mile trek homeward with the long narrow head-baskets full of kola-nuts destined for the markets of Tunis, Tripoli and Khartoum. Those baskets, called *bankaia*, are exactly the same to-day as they were described a thousand years ago by the Arab authors. African Africa does not change. Now there comes running and singing and shouting a band of young men, almost naked, with only a loin-cloth of white native-made cotton. These are men coming south to earn some money at the mines, or "sell their hoes" as they term it, which means to work on the Ashanti farms. Here is a line of their brothers returning —clothed, and generally with a small iron chest on the head, containing presents for the folk at home and odd trifles picked up during its owner's sojourn in the south. Now a flock of sheep and goats trotting briskly along, now and then nibbling at the vegetation which banks the road. They do not seem tired or weary, yet they have been driven some seven hundred miles perhaps, and to-day is their last long trek, for at Coomassie they will be killed or sent by train to the hungry mining camps; their herdsmen, tall, semi-nude, silent men, are armed with a spear or bow and arrows, lest a lion or a hyæna should attack the flock.

Not far away is a herd of cattle crossing the road—the cattle-track does not lie along the motor-road, for this last would soon be ruined by the thousands of head of cattle which make, after rain, a morass whenever they pass. What a picturesque fellow is leading them—long-haired, wild-looking. He comes from the desert's edge and is of some slave caste. His master follows the herd, a fine Arab-featured man; he walks like a king and is obviously one who knows not fear. His race? No man here knows. He belongs to the Niger Valley.

Here comes a pair of wandering troubadours with crude instruments in their hands—calabashes covered with iguana skin and stringed triply with horsehair. They will earn money at their trade wherever they go, for they know the art of flattery. I once knew a soldier to give two of them five shillings—four whole days' pay—because they ran by his side, danced before him, shouting out "Lion! Lion!" It is a common trait in the black man, this love of flattery, this vanity. Many Government clerks never save, even when they are stationed in the most out-of-the-way districts. They keep open house, and give money freely to all and sundry, especially the flattering, honey-tongued musician.

Such is the road. It fell to my lot to have the privilege of connecting our section with that in French territory, so that motors can now run almost throughout the year from Coomassie to the Sudan. To-day, therefore, in addition to these thousands on foot, one sees scores of cars of all sorts and, *mirabile dictu*, some that are not unlike buses and chars-à-bancs. But the road itself is a very old one indeed, and lies to-day substantially along the same route as it did in the days when Portugal sent her ambassadors to the Na of Moshi.

Of the country one passes through there is not much to write. For some forty miles one passes through the great forest, the road a narrow strip of red between the liane-adorned green and black-green trees. Here and there is a village or a town; children and sheep and dogs and long-snouted pigs flying helter-skelter at one's approach. Modernism is triumphant; black-and-white oblong houses verandahed and corrugated-iron roofed. Native villages are to be met with only off the track to-day.

There is a rather fine piece of scenery among the hills just south of Mampong. The road climbs these, curving upward and upward, with cliffs and precipices on either side. The view is ever-changing, and there are one or two really beautiful glimpses across the sea of tree-tops, broken here and there with wisps of mist rising from invisible streams. But one does not come as yet to West Africa for scenery.

Soon after Mampong one begins to leave the forest.

The trees rapidly grow less tall; new varieties are met with, until quite suddenly one finds oneself in a forest with grass growing between the trees, not our grass, but tall reeds six feet or more high. And then equally imperceptibly one is in a grass country all bespattered with trees, a badly kept, over-stocked orchard. Here and there one will see a thicket, a last remnant of the primeval forest.

With this change come many others. We reach Ejura—no longer a parody of a modern town, no longer rectangular houses, no longer an Ashanti town. The huts are round, beehive-shaped, grass-covered; sheep and goats are far more numerous; there is a feel of openness; the sticky dampness of the forest is gone; the oppressive smell of rotting vegetation is no longer, in its place is the overpowering pungency (euphemism for "beastly smell") of locust-bean cakes, worse far than that of sun-dried fish—stink-fish we call it. There are horses here too, and plenty of cattle. Ejura is a large centre of trade; it is the last town in the open country, where every caravan halts before it enters the forest.

One passes Ejura to-day, but one used to halt here and proceed on foot as soon as enough carriers had been collected. There was nothing of interest in this; it was a prosaic business. The men were not new to the work, being permanently engaged men, mostly of the Mendi tribe from Sierra Leone. They more or less chose their own loads and stuck to them for the remainder of the trek—six to seven days' march—to Salaga. Wonderful men they were too; they would do a twenty-four-mile trek with sixty pounds at least on their heads, and arrive at the trot. Of course they were looters in a small way, picking up trifles whenever they could. But the black man expects that, and provided this petty thieving and extortion is moderate, no complaints are ever made.

I was not alone on this, my first, trek to the north, another European coming up with me, which made the march far from wearisome. We had a little pigeon- and partridge-shooting, but otherwise nothing, for the rains were not yet over and the grass was very high. Moreover the floods were out, and that year was a record one. For miles one splashed through water, often waist-high. The passage of rivers was difficult, possibly dangerous. Streams which in the dry season are without water and look like rather large ditches spread over the country on either side for several hundred yards, the stream itself an ugly-looking spate; others are of the torrent variety and some are even impassable. Fortunately they fall rapidly.

One has many adventures at times when on trek during the rains, and the methods of passage across rivers are varied. Some one must swim, others one can just manage to walk across; others again have hollowed-out tree-trunks, called dug-outs, to carry one over. These last are rarely straight, and difficult to handle. Sometimes again there are so-called native bridges; usually a fallen tree serves to walk on, and a loose stretch of liana acts as handrail. The foothold more often than not is below the surface of the water. In a rushing, boiling, yellow-coloured spate such a passage is not pleasant.

Again, one finds methods far less ordinary. There are gourds in which one sits huddled up, grasping one's knees just as one does in cock-fighting. You sit like that and a local native *au courant* of the currents swims behind and propels you across. Or if the local gourds are not large enough to provide a bath-like receptacle sufficient for a man, the natives just hollow out the gourds, and rivet into place the portion cut out of the rind after the inside has been scooped out. The gourd then floats, and you hug it, dangling your legs, possibly your body, in the water, and so get propelled across. When gourds are entirely lacking, bundles of dry grass are sewn into a skin of a cow, making as it were a *pouf*, and one either sits on it or hugs it, with the human propeller behind. Personally I generally strip and swim, but all one's loads are carried across in the above precarious manner.

But there are streams either too swift to swim or too wooded on the banks to permit of landing. It is then advisable to leave the passage entirely to the local natives. They have all sorts of ingenious methods of seeing that you and your loads get across in safety. The most exciting method I ever encountered was in the Nankanni country. There had been three days of very heavy downpour, but as these were the first rains, and all the streams till then had been bone-dry, I did not expect a large stream—rivers are not named in the north, for until recently no man was wont to travel sufficiently far to find others than his own local one—to be seriously affected, neither did my carriers, all local men. However, when we reached its banks it was in full flood and passage absolutely impossible. The water was at least thirty feet deep, about forty yards across, and on the opposite bank only tree-tops were visible. The stream itself was racing and eddying in a very ugly manner. We camped on the left bank that night, the carriers eating a reed-buck I chanced to shoot. That shot was lucky. It attracted the attention of some men on the opposite bank, and they shouted across to my men to know who we were. They promised to tell their chief and to return in the morning.

Early next day the people arrived on the opposite side and said they would get us across all right; but it would take some time and would I try to get them a "meat." I failed in this and returned in about two hours. Most of my loads were already across, and I arrived to see the balance being taken. The people had cut a lot of thin sticks into about seven-foot lengths, tied them in pairs and lashed these right across the river among the tree-tops, where they completely arched the water. As a greater precaution they themselves had climbed into the branches, forming thereby an endless chain, passing men and loads from one to the other. It was a really fine piece of ingenuity. I do not think any European would have trusted such slender branches, let alone have stationed close on two hundred men among them over a boiling flood, for there was not the slightest chance of saving anyone had he slipped. Some months later I crossed the same river dryshod. I went to see the native bridge. It was actually about thirty-five feet above the bed of the river and less than five feet from the tops of the trees.

There was an amusing passage of a small but deep and rapid stream not far from Wuyai on the Dakar river. One native of the village, and only one, was able to swim or get across. He held a rope attached to one end of a dug-out. And such a dug-out! It was so small that I could not even sit in it, and could take only one box at a time. The other end was also attached to a rope, and the passage was made shuttlecock fashion.

On my first trip north the floods were very bad indeed, and we nearly lost one carrier, who persisted in crossing a stream with a load on his head. He could not swim but contented himself with walking across. The water was above his head, and our attention was drawn to his two arms extended over his head holding up the load. I suppose the weight held him down. We had to go to his help, and my companion, an M.O., had to attend him on his coming ashore. I do not know how one can walk across a river when out of one's depth, but I saw a similar incident in North Togoland. The man was the Government interpreter, and he refused assistance across. Having stripped, he walked into the water, holding his clothes in a bundle over his head. He had carefully oriented himself before starting, but when half-way across lost direction and quite gaily proceeded downstream. There was another European with me, and we could not refrain from laughter; we had him rescued in time.

Eventually we reached Salaga. I stopped only a couple of nights to change carriers, for here the regular transport used to end and men were sent down from one's future district to take one up. Salaga used to be a well-known slave-mart. It was the great emporium of the south and the north, and its name is used in many proverbs of the northern folk. "To go to Salaga" was almost an equivalent of our own "to go to Jericho." But in the late eighties the Gonja rulers (for Salaga was the commercial capital of that tribe) were at war with each other over the succession to the paramount chieftainship. That war ruined the town, and several years before our advent into the country Salaga had been replaced in importance by a mart farther to the west, known as Kintampo.

Traces of its pristine glory are, however, everywhere apparent. For the last two hours' march into the place one follows a dead-straight road running through a treeless expanse, an area almost entirely denuded by man, who has been in search of farmlands and, later, firewood. It is a most dreary approach, and being at the end of a long march is even more than usually wearisome. The native path was of course not a straight one, but when I first came there a good wide road had been cut and constructed, the present motor-road. It is excellent for motors, but for walking it is execrable. And then, to cap all, Salaga, visible for two hours in its cluster of kapok and other tall trees, planted years ago for shade, is not the end of the march. It is nearly half-an-hour farther to the station—the longest, most tiring thirty minutes imaginable. I was almost done in with the heat and the march. The D.C. met me, and at once remarked: "Isn't that a really fine road of mine!"

There is nothing remarkable about this once well-known town. It holds about three thousand people altogether, and is a conglomeration of round mud huts more or less set at haphazard (the huts are grouped together into compounds, a series of huts being linked by mud walls); grass roofs, several shade trees, numbers of covered water-holes, red-earth streets and alleyways; sheep and goats and children playing about; here and there white-clothed Sudanese. There is a so-called mosque. (I do not know why we always in West Africa use grandiose terms; it is misleading.) These mosques are mud affairs modelled roughly on the lines of the Mahdi's tomb, but very small—only about thirty feet high. The dome is all stuck about, like cakes with almonds, with projecting beams. The whole is more or less squared off on the outside, and usually at each corner is stuck an ostrich egg. These buildings certainly strike one amidst the sameness of the round huts. But there are very few—possibly throughout the whole Protectorate there are not ten, for Mohammedanism here has never made the slightest progress, the Dagomba confederation having been throughout the centuries a firm bulwark against the influence of Islam.

From Salaga to Yendi, my first destination, is a march of five days through very sparsely inhabited bush. Nothing of note is to be expected, but before the rains set in one can get quite good hunting just alongside the road.

Yendi is in Togoland, and administered under mandate from the League of Nations by Great Britain. It is the capital of the Dagomba kingdom and dwelling-place of the Na—the native title of their paramount ruler. The town is of the usual sort, a conglomeration of round mud huts linked into compounds. But the number of trees, lofty and dark-leafed, is noteworthy. One crosses several miles of treeless country, almost farmed out. The sun is very strong and marching is dusty and hot; but in front is the town of Yendi, obviously cool and shady. The market-place is so shaded that no sun at all filters through.

This bareness of the country is typical throughout the

Dagomba kingdom. Long and undisturbed settlement enabled the people to farm in peace and to a greater extent than those unfortunates who dwelt in troubled lands. The system of cultivation is very destructive of tree life. When an area is chosen by a man for cultivation, his first step is to ring-bark all those trees which are useless to him. Thus he will save shea-butter-trees and other fruit-bearing varieties, and actually for a few years increase their productivity by working the soil at their roots. After the ring-barking he will hoe up all the weeds and grass, let them dry and burn them. Usually he will plant yams the first year. This is done by making mounds of earth into which seed yams are set. Yams are climbers, and the ring-barked trees serve that year as growing poles. The following year most of these are either felled or blown down during tornadoes. By the time the field is exhausted no timber remains at all, and only a very coarse sour grass can grow. At the same time weathering has filled in the hoe-ruts with dust and sand, to which wind-borne sand is added. Naturally, by erosion, heat and cold, dryness and heavy rain, more and more sand is created, until gradually the country is becoming sand, and in some hundred years or so will probably become desert, unless steps, now being considered, prove effective in staving off this disaster.

Salaga, Yendi, all these towns show this dearth of trees. I remarked how this was due to a great extent to the fact that they had been long settled and had enjoyed a peaceful government. Perhaps nowhere in West Africa has there ever been so powerful and so peaceful an empire as that of the Dagomba. To a very large extent the great kingdom has been overlooked by European writers. I have in my custody a manuscript of the history of the country as remembered by the natives themselves, and I hope at a future date to be in a position to edit it.

The Dagomba rulers maintain a Court very similar to the vulgarly accepted type of the Orient, but it differs in that the buildings are exceedingly mean and lowly—no stone palaces, no minarets, no fountains in marble courtyards, but there are harems, viziers, eunuchs. The ruler is called Na. His position is an hereditary one to a certain extent. All the ruling class are of one tribe, the people of another. The blood royal can descend to the peasantry, but the latter cannot rise to a throne.

Tradition goes back a thousand years, and, as usual, to one man, who is distinguished not by his personal beauty but by an appalling loathsomeness—a leprous, deformed, filthy creature, whose prowess in war is enhanced by the terror his ugliness inspires. The first of these conquerors came and seized the kingship, and by intermarriage with the people finally established a dominant position. Their rule, though despotic, was undoubtedly a benevolent one. The country was never devastated by war, and never again subdued. Population increased. Even the rulers became too numerous. They fared forth and carved for themselves new kingdoms, modelled on this parent one. These were the three great Moshi kingdoms, which, with those of Dagomba and Mamprussi, formed a federation of kingdoms, which resisted all invasions of the Moorish and other tribes of the desert. So powerful was this kingdom or group of kingdoms that their soldiery twice destroyed Timbuktu, and their friendship and alliance was sought for in the interests of Christianity by the Portuguese in the early years of the sixteenth century.

But this federation broke before European might in the scramble for Africa, and the lands were divided between the three Powers—Germany, France and ourselves. At Yendi resides the Na of the Dagomba, who by the event of the war has seen his fathers' kingdom once again made one.

I was at Yendi when his father died, and the following is taken from a description of the events I wrote in *Man*:

"On 19th January 1917, Alasan (the Na) died suddenly during the national festival of *damba*, the harvest-home of the yam and cereal crops. His death was announced to me in these words: 'Our eyes are red.' It was but three A.M., and I naturally was somewhat hasty at the disturbance of my slumbers, and to my query as to what it meant, the answer came: 'We have now no more honour.' The interpreter deemed it advisable to explain that he thought the messenger meant their king was dead. They then asked for permission to beat 'their big drum,' so that all men should know of the misfortune. At the same time the beating of this drum would notify the chief of Bagale that his master is dead. This is necessary, since he is the hereditary guardian of the house whither kings' souls go after death. It consists of one hut only, which I was told has never been allowed to fall into disrepair, and was erected over the tomb of a former ruler, one Sitogo. As soon as the chief of Bagale hears the drumming, he takes a pot and places it inside the door of this house with water and corn in it. He leaves the door open and retires again. The soul can then enter and eat. The chief of Bagale's senior wife must close the door before morning, and may never sleep with her husband again. Bagale is a good hundred miles from Yendi as the crow flies.

"Ordinarily, the king's death is kept secret by the ministers of the Crown (eunuchs) and elders of Yendi, but when Alasan died there was in his hut one of his wives, and she ran out immediately and began throwing her property over the wall of the royal compound, lest it should be seized by the king's servants. Other wives realized what had happened; and the news soon spread throughout the compound, so that the chief eunuch was obliged to publish it abroad.

"The messengers draw rein outside the compound of the chief to whom they have been sent and call out that they have ill tidings. The people of the compound come out, and recognizing the messenger, endeavour to catch him. He must seek sanctuary at the market-place, for, if caught, he can regain his freedom only by being ransomed by his family. Should he reach refuge he is called back and gives the message: 'The king has gone to his farm.'

"The grave is in the king's own compound, and in a special hut wherein he may not enter during his lifetime. When the body is being carried to this burial hut a cow is slaughtered on the way thereto, and across its body is carried the king's corpse. All who have been faithful to the king, or have had no sexual intercourse with any of his wives, touch the animal's blood and rub it on their forehead, or dip a kola-nut in it and chew it. The meat is cooked and eaten. This is an ordeal, for everyone who has touched one of the king's wives would surely die when partaking of the meat. Even if unawares he receives a piece of the meat, death will find him out. The remainder is roasted and kept as an ingredient for the ordeal poison.

" Immediately the king is buried his wives gather by the grave and renew their lamentations, and this they do whenever a chief arrives, for about a month or so, when, too, the heads of all the king's children are shaved. But before this the king's own children are numbered, grandchildren and bastards being excluded.

" On the third night after the shaving, the chief of Gukpiogo, who is on this occasion called the chief of the dead, will come at midnight with his followers, all of them walking stark naked to the grave of their king, and it is said that on their arrival all the ghosts of the dead kings of Yendi will be present. Twice they run round the compound in which the corpse of the king is buried; they then enter it and satisfy themselves that all has been done correctly. Consequences most dire would follow if anyone attempted to look at them, so proclamation of their visit is made on the two evenings before their arrival; and after dark no one goes out, nor is any sound made, for not even may a dog bark and live. After the visit they withdraw secretly.

" And on the last day of the funeral a horse, a donkey and a dog are slain for the departed king's service.

" The house over the grave is then knocked down, the ruins being left one year. They are then cleared away, the grave is opened, and men stir the bones with sticks.

The stakes which closed the tomb are knocked down, and the hole is filled with the excavated earth. Above this is placed a stone, a brass pan standing on it. These pans may still be found in many places; but in Yendi they are gone, and only the stones mark the various royal graves."

The process of king-making is extremely interesting, and contains undoubtedly many survivals of a far more ancient regime than that of the present ruling family. It did not fall to my lot to be at Yendi when the new Na was chosen. The rules for this are very definite ones. A Na must be himself the son of a Na, a real son, not grandson, and he must have reached by promotion the rank next to that of Na. Three such offices exist: the chieftainships of Karaga, Savelugu and Miong. The actual selection is made by the *tindana* (a sort of priest, *lit.* "owner of the earth") of Gushiego, who acts under the advice of the other chieftains, and especially that of the corps of eunuchs. The one selected is informed, and after suitable preparation spends the last day before assuming power as a slave, and is beaten, spat on and otherwise abused. That evening the *tindana* takes him into the hut where are kept the staves of all the former Nas. He is told to choose one. The room is dark and he must perforce select at haphazard. His choice is hurriedly glanced at. If it is the staff of a good Na, he will be a good Na, if that of a bad chief, then he too will be a bad chief.

Of course in former times, as one can well imagine, the rivalry between the three candidates more often than not led to civil wars, which do not seem to have done much harm to the country as a whole. During these periods of unrest, power was in the hands of the eunuchs.

These men were all slaves, captives taken in war. The good-looking boys—good looks are usually a sign of intelligence among the natives—were set aside, and at the proper season (about April) were sent to one of the villages where the ceremony of eunuchization was allowed by the local deity—for that is, as a rule, a deed hateful to the earth-gods. The children were rendered unconscious by being ceaselessly flicked in the face with the hairs of a cow's tail. The operation over, specially prepared shea-butter was put on the wound. Of course this is not now tolerated: there are no longer any slaves and one does not eunuchize free boys. I was told that comparatively few boys died as a result of the operation.

The young eunuchs then entered a sort of college, where they were trained in various arts and crafts pertaining to the Na's house and town. From ordinary household slaves they could and did rise to the highest position in the land, and finally reached a small body of men who actually ruled the kingdom and who were so highly held in esteem that they could contradict the Na, differ from his views and even abuse him.

There is an immense wealth of customary laws and folklore to be tapped at Yendi. It is a district where one's work used to be done alone and in intimate relation with the people. The loneliness (to-day there are three or four Europeans stationed there) was somewhat trying, for during the dry season the scenery is appalling in its monotonous colouring—black ashes and brown leafless trees.

There are some queer stories told of the results of loneliness on men. Undoubtedly one loses one's sense of proportion and becomes somewhat unbalanced; and the effect of meeting one's fellow white men after months of isolation is twofold. One rapidly thaws out, after a preliminary frosty first half-hour, and becomes almost intoxicated with excitement. That is the mental effect. One's brain is in a turmoil; rest is impossible: in bed one goes over and over again the conversation, and thinks out new opinions, fresh arguments. Physically the effect is curious. There are throat muscles, of which one was quite unaware before. These are not used, apparently, except for the subdued tones customary to our conversation with our kin.

Solitude affects men in different ways. I knew of one who used to potter about his house all day, save when at work, and his sole recreation was to study a Bradshaw and a clergy-list. The former enabled him to work out weird cross-country trips; the latter amused him by trying to conjure up from the names of the livings and the incumbents pictures of their life! Another used to have a paper sent out daily from home. These he would arrange in order of date on their arrival in the mail and hand the bundle to a small boy, whose duty it was each morning, after his master had risen, to run up the path shouting: "Pia-pa! Pai-pa!" The man then shouted out: "Boy, boy! Bring me a paper." The boy handed him the top paper—six weeks behind in time—and received for it one penny. That penny was placed by his master's bedside for use next morning. On Sundays a Sabbath paper replaced the daily one.

A third I knew thought he had a sense of humour, and he was always up to some far-fetched jest. Once there came out a General Order to the effect that European bungalows were to be either named or numbered. Obviously this order was intended for towns where the European population was considerable, and not for stations where there was only one European, who combined in himself the offices of postmaster and postman. However, he acted on the order and had a signpost painted on which was "ZCHZCH VILLA." This was at the time of Przemysl. When he knew his senior officer was coming to inspect the station he had this sign erected in a conspicuous place. All worked according to plan. The S.O. was rather a "livery" man and did not like jokes. He saw the sign and demanded:

"What the devil's that?"

"The name of my house, sir, in accordance with G.O."

"And how the devil do you pronounce it?" roared the S.O.

Plagiarizing Mark Twain, he replied:

"Some, sir, call it Marjoribanks; others, Cholmondeley. I myself say 'Pouf.'"

He told me the effect of the jest was all that he had imagined, and it was successful beyond measure.

Yendi is a very important station. Being the capital of the Dagomba kingdom this is but natural. However, the Dagomba are as a tribe one of the most peaceful and law-abiding. Serious crime is absent, save with very rare exceptions, and civil cases are nearly always settled satisfactorily by the chiefs. Of course there is a certain amount of bribery and corruption, but less than one would expect to meet. One could write a treatise on the subject, for to these people, as to Eastern people, justice is obviously a purchasable item, and when one comes to think carefully on this matter one will soon see that after all it is not so very evil when universal.

The Dagomba, therefore, do not affect one much in one's work. The importance of the district lies in the fact that it encloses within its area the country of an untamed tribe called the Konkomba. It is a curious fact that all over the Moshi- or Dagomba-ruled countries one will find islands of anarchy. It is possible that these untamed tribes are remnants of the people who resided where the Dagomba do now, and who fled into tracts where those conquerors could not come. For it is undoubtedly due to the use of horses and clothing that the Dagomba and Moshi owed, in the first instance, their victories; for with horses they were superior in mobility to the naked warriors, and with loose clothing they were to a certain extent protected from the small arrows used by the local people.

These islands of unconquered peoples provided in the past permanent reservoirs for slave-hunting, and by far the greater number of slaves shipped from the Gold Coast were of this stock. Slave-raiding ceased only a quarter of a century ago.

The Konkomba form one of these reservoirs. They are magnificent savages, and every year to this day they indulge in a little blood-letting—that is to say, there is an annual intervillage war. Of course we eventually put a stop to this; but as one never knows where a fight will take place this custom cannot, until the people learn better, be absolutely ended.

These wars arise almost invariably over a woman and, because the vendetta obtains throughout, are almost interminable, reviving each year during the season when, owing to the dryness, work in the fields is slack. Not only among the Konkomba but among all the isolated tribes this custom prevails, but is not quite so vigorous as it is with the former. Curiously enough the wars are revived by the womenfolk, who will taunt a young man in public at the markets with leaving the blood of some relative unavenged.

If the taunts are levelled at an individual, a murder will result; if at a village, a small war. Usually casualties are not numerous, but the percentage of fatal wounds is high, as the arrows used are poisoned with strophanthus.

At the beginning of the first rains all the villages collect their strophanthus. The young men erect shelters, apart from the compounds, of grass mats; the strophanthus seeds are prepared, fowls sacrificed, and the poison brewed. This lasts a couple of days. During that time no stranger may approach the brewing-place: the young men may not sleep in their compounds, but must remain beside the poison; women may not be touched—they may not even bring their menfolk food, only one aged dame from each compound doing this, nor may they come near the place. It is a serious occasion, and there is no laughter in the matter.

When the brew is ready, and the arrows properly smeared, company-hunting is indulged in to test the strength of the poison. Many villages join for the occasion.

The animals killed are awarded scrupulously to him whose arrow is found embedded in them, even if found long after and far away near other villages—a contrast to the usual habit of slaying and eating any cattle, even of one's friend, which may stray into one's own pasturage.

Once I witnessed a fight between two villages, but was too far off to follow the tactics. It was viewed from a scarp looking over a treeless plain where the two villages were at war. Someone saw our horses; the battle ended. Both sides came up the cliff to interview me and to explain that the other side had attacked them first.

These wars are very numerous, and sometimes a village will destroy all the huts, burn the corn-bins of the rivals, and carry off the cattle, sheep and other live stock. At times they are carried on in a rather treacherous fashion. The village or settlement of Kugnani had been invited to attend the funeral custom of an old man who had died at a near-by village. Now they knew that there was certain to be invited also a party from the village of Libopale, with whom there was a vendetta; but no attack was expected owing to the protection given magically on such occasions. Twelve men were sent, and when they arrived they greeted the family of the deceased and then went off to visit their friends until the wake was started. As soon as they had scattered, the Libopale men arrived, began to abuse and mock at one of the Kugnani, and eventually began to shoot their arrows. The war-cry was raised, and the wretched Kugnani had to run for it, as they had very few arrows and those unpoisoned. Of the twelve, nine

A Konkomba Maid.

Note the cicatrices all over her body. She is girded with European beads in many strings knotted together in front in a cluster of cowries.

were killed and the other three wounded. The incident actually took place on French soil, but both villages concerned were British. Curiously enough the Kugnani, although considerably superior in strength, did not "eat up" Libopale. They came to me. I presume that had they attacked their enemies other vendettas would have been remembered, and Kugnani would have brought on itself much trouble.

That treacherous attack had come as a result of women mocking the young men of Libopale at the great market of Sambul, where also I traced a second variety of vendetta, cold-blooded murder by the individual. A young man went to the market to sell some fowls. He strolled over to the beer-stalls (beer made from millet) and chatted with the girls selling it. One of them apparently did not like him, and told him so in as many words, adding that anyway he was not a man, as his grandfather's blood was still on the ground.

The youth said nothing save that he would show that he was a man, and returned to his village. There he made the necessary preparations and marked down his victim, an elderly man, who, owing to the vendetta, had moved off into the bush, where he had built for himself and his wife a couple of huts, and where he considered he was safe from vengeance.

The distance from the youth's village to his victim's house was about forty-five miles. He covered this and waited for nightfall. Then he approached the door of the hut with a bundle of straw as a torch. This he set down in front of the door, but apparently the man inside did not awake. Usually a mud screen is erected in every hut as a precaution against just such events as these, but unfortunately this had been left undone. The youth, on removing the grass-mat door, could see his victim asleep, and, shouting his war-cry, shot three arrows into him, killing him at once.

However, the excitement of the deed and its great success were his undoing. He lost his head and himself got lost. (This is not infrequent among these highly strung people, and is of course attributed to magic.) He was found next day wandering aimlessly about in a bewildered state, and was duly brought to justice.

More often than not these vendetta murders cannot be brought home to their perpetrators, and I suppose it is a custom that will die out only in the course of time. One of these murders, which justice never was able to avenge, occurred in the Builsa country. It serves to show how difficult it is to punish the criminal.

About six o'clock one morning I saw a youth clasping the flag-pole outside my bungalow at Navaro. This was a general custom among the people when they were particularly anxious to bring their troubles to the white man. I therefore sent for him and asked what was the matter.

He informed me that he had come from a place called Uassi, thirty miles away; that he had travelled all night, and that he had witnessed a terrible crime, for he had seen an old man murdered. His story was an apparently straightforward one. It appeared that he had been over to Wiaga, and on his way back home he had decided to have a bathe. A good stream crossed the path and he went up it a little way. Scarcely had he entered the water than he heard voices, which he recognized as being those of two of the sons of the chief of Wiaga. He listened to them arranging the details for the murder of an old man, named Aloja.

I asked him if he knew any motive, and he said: "Oh yes; everyone knows they want his wife." He continued that he was frightened and had remained very quiet, but that when they had gone on he had followed to see what they would do.

Now on that same day there was being held at a village along the Wiaga and Uassi path an important funeral custom, to which most of the countryside had been invited. There was therefore plenty of traffic, and the boy could have got assistance had he thought about it. However he did not, but said he followed the pair to the funeral custom and had then watched them until nightfall, when they made off to Aloja's house.

Arrived there he heard them call out Aloja, and when the old man emerged they hit him over the head with an axe. The youth had then run away, and had come straight to the white man, who did not like such things.

The story sounded all right, so I sent off the sergeant and a couple of men to bring in the corpse and the two accused youths. So rapid were the constables that they reached the corpse before even the chiefs concerned knew of the murder and arrested the youths while they were still at the funeral custom. The wife of the victim was also brought along.

The two suspected youths—one was only about fifteen years old—denied all knowledge of the event, stating that they had ridden over to the wake and had been there the whole time. Several hundred witnesses could prove that.

The corpse was still quite fresh. Aloja had been killed with an axe, the blade of which was still in the head. The blow must have been a very severe one for this to happen. The axes are fixed on to V-shaped handles, one arm of which is pointed and driven into the shaft of the blade. Therefore the harder one hits, the more securely is the head forced on.

The informant's story was thus to a certain extent borne out; but the motive had gone, for Aloja's wife was blood-sister to the two accused. Moreover she had been present at the murder.

She told how everyone had gone to the wake, only herself and the old man remaining at home. Shortly after dark she heard a man calling: "Aloja! Aloja!" He had answered: "What do you want?" The man had replied that he could not find the path to Flambissi. Aloja had gone out to show it him. She had then heard the war-cry and had rushed out. She could not see much at first, as it was dark and she had been in front of a fire, but she made out the body of her husband.

"Aloja! Aloja!" she had cried, "what is it?"

And he had replied: "Anam has done this thing. To-day my fathers call me." And so saying he died.

The woman had dragged him back into the hut and had waited for the people to come back. The first she saw were the constables!

Now Anam was a very old man indeed. He lived about two miles from the scene of the murder and he was so old that he could not even walk. He had not done so for several months prior to the murder. But there was a connecting link between Anam and Aloja. The latter's father had killed Anam's brother, whose son was the father to the youth, my informant.

When Aloja died he named Anam as his murderer, not meaning that Anam had done this deed, but that as he was the head of his family he therefore was responsible for everything done by members of that family, and therefore he indicated which family was responsible.

But Anam had two grand-nephews, Akande, who was my informant, and his brother Alanjo. The latter was missing.

I detained Akande for some time, hoping to effect Alanjo's arrest, but the latter never reappeared. There was no further evidence except that the girls at the market-place had "ragged" both Akande and Alanjo over the unavenged blood. I had to release Akande, and shortly after came home on leave. On my return I asked what had become of Akande, and was informed: "Oh! he became a member of the Murderers' Society; he cleansed himself of the ghost and has left for French territory." He had shown himself wearing the insignia of a cleansed murderer and had then gone off. Alanjo had not been seen.

Throughout all the north and north-eastern half of the Protectorate are to be found these murderers' societies or associations. Konkomba, Lobi, Grunshi, Dagati, Builsa—all of them have these clubs, and the initiation ceremonies often contain what seem remnants of former cannibalism, for until quite recent times the liver of the slain was smoked and dried, and after being pulverized was mixed with certain herbs into a concoction which was shared by all the other slayers of men as well as the novice. Details differ somewhat, and it is, of course, difficult to discuss such matters. Little distinction is made between murderers and slayers of men in genuine warfare. The slayers have to go through the same ceremonies of purification, perform the same sacrifices; nor does the general weight of public opinion protest against such crimes as yet. That takes time. Public opinion on points such as these differs from tribe to tribe, and an interesting case of this came to my notice among the Konkomba.

There had been a lot of fighting, and two villages especially had shown great activity in this warfare. I therefore disarmed them, destroying several thousands of arrows. The people then naïvely asked me what they would do when their late opponents attacked them. I pointed out that their quarrels would be my quarrels, etc., etc., and went away.

Some few days later five youths came to me from these villages and complained that on the preceding day all their womenfolk had been kidnapped on their way back from a market.

The women were restored some four days later. They were asked by me if they had any complaints, to which they replied they had none. So they returned home. A few days later a youth came and asked me whether, since his promised wife had been raped whilst kidnapped, the child would be his. I then saw all the women again and asked them if they had been raped. Their spokeswoman, an aged dame, said: "Of course!" I asked why they had not complained and if they had resisted. She answered: "Women do not resist men, for they have whips. We do not complain when the shea-butter-tree has fruit."

CHAPTER VII

TORNADOES—FISHING

TREKKING in the Northern Territories is to a new-comer of great interest. Used to the forest with no views, with scarcely any form of life save that of insects, with dampness and steamy heat, suddenly long ranges of mountains break upon one's vision, life of all sorts is close by, and there is a dry and not unpleasant warmth, though during some months the heat is intense. But after a while trekking loses much of its charm. The scenery is monotonous, miles and miles of undulating grass country covered with small trees making the whole like a very badly kept, and worse-planted, orchard or park. Rarely is this broken save when one descends to a river or stream where there are great meadows, fair enough to look on, but most evil to tread, as the earth is rarely flat and even, but either humpy or broken by crevices to a depth of a foot or more, and about the same in width. Off the track one can always be certain of seeing a herd of kob or roan, or some wart-hog rooting.

When the early rains set in, plant-life is at its best. The trees have cast their brown, scorched leaves, and have garbed themselves in various greens, most extravagant of hue; but in the far north, where the "bush" has been completely absorbed for the requirements of man, the trees are usually of the camel-thorn variety, and bear a blue-green foliage during the dry season, throughout the rains remaining quite bare. Their tall gaunt forms provide a striking contrast to the surrounding greenery.

But there are some spots where wild flowers thrive, and bespangle the young grass with their whites and yellows and blues. Great lilies, white with crimson splashes, peep above the new grass; bushes are all ablaze with wild gardenias; or tall ground-orchids are clustered together, their spikes a mass of gold or mauve or white; groups of great bushes, almost trees, are laden with purple or yellow or scarlet flowers; shrubs with great tendrils, several feet long, are a mass of glaring vermilion; all these reward the traveller as he toils along the well-known paths. Once I stumbled on a veritable garden, a playground where the hand of God Himself alone had laboured. It was in Ashanti. I wandered up a stretch of bare rock to obtain a view of the country, when I suddenly found myself in a wondrous spot. The rock had been broken and had formed itself into a series of nullahs. These were quite wide and deep, with ponds and pools of translucent water (very rare indeed in West Africa). They were banked with veritable lawns of a mosslike grass, which were bordered with clumps of a gigantic sweet-smelling lily, virgin-white, with an odour of peaches. Dark-leafed shrubs, a mass of creamy balls, gave forth the sweetness of frangipanni. Here and there a fernlike palm stood erect amidst a group of nondescript shrubs which were gashed with long branches all blood-red from myriads of minute blossoms. I could have dallied long amidst these nullahs, for they were numerous and asked to be explored and admired. I should have loved to bathe in the pools, and bask and dry on the lawns. But it was West Africa, and a couple of large snakes hissed at me and warned me off their preserves.

That was in the beginning of the rains; but it is not always then that the flowers thrive. In the dry season there are gladioli of a weird colour—mauve and green and yellow mixed together as in a cotton print. There are fields of giant African daisies, sunlike in their glaring gold. There are scores of beautiful rock-plants, which mass together and, though minute in themselves, in their numbers make a veritable carpet of blue or yellow or pink; wild portluca, pink and yellow; a sort of crocus, yellow and white and mauve; and a botanical curiosity in white that flowers for a day and reminds one of a narcissus or a daffodil. All these beauties of nature fascinate the eye and gladden the soul. Someone once told me that there were no flowers in West Africa!

But in scenery the country is certainly poor. There is so little variety; even when one can obtain a distant view the horizon is unbroken; the undulations are not apparent; it is deadly monotonous. I once remarked on this to a European and he replied: "Yes, the view is there; but if only one could see a village, a church spire, a tower, it would be beautiful."

There are one or two exceptions to this continuous dullness and sameness. In the north-east corner there are ranges of hills, which—so strange are they to the eye, since so unaccustomed—we call mountains. Even Binger, the great explorer, who first of all white men penetrated there, was so struck with the height that he reported the Peak of Nauri as being close on four thousand feet. Actually it is less than one thousand, but so flat and unbroken is the country that one can easily be mistaken.

All through the districts of Zuaragu and Bawku are small ranges of these hills, bare and rocky. Some are massive piles of granite, weathered into fantastic shapes; others are of a sort of schist, which crops out almost at right angles to the ground and gives an appearance of hundreds of ill-dressed and haphazardly arranged tombstones. All this country is under cultivation, with very few places not yet absorbed, and when one enters the area round Nangodi one is struck by a resemblance to the Rhineland: terraces running right to the summit of the hills remind one of the vineyards.

But the principal break in the landscape is the scarp which runs from the north-east of the Protectorate for about a hundred and fifty miles, more or less regularly, with but few breaks, in a direction somewhat south of west. This scarp at places rears itself eight hundred feet above the surrounding country almost precipitously, and there are comparatively few passes through it. The scarp faces inland, and I suppose marked at one time the left bank of a river which has since been absorbed into the Volta, in the same way as this latter has actually stolen some of the Niger waters in recent times.

The country round the scarp is teeming with game of all sorts, and lion are common in consequence. The scenery is wild and rough, and seen at a distance the scarp has a really fine appearance of cliffs—chalk cliffs being conjured up when the setting sun lights up the rock face and makes it a dazzling white. But a nearer view is not so fine, and the precipitousness of the ridge becomes less and less as one begins to focus the outlines of the foothills.

One cannot say, however, that really fine scenery exists on the Gold Coast, but possibly one might allow of such an epithet to the southern portion of the area of Togoland—mandated to Great Britain—especially in the district of Krachi, where the country is of the open bush variety, and one can get views over wide areas. Here the eastern frontier is a range of mountains, thickly afforested at their base, but ending in grass and bare rock. They rise to about three thousand feet above sea-level, and are very steep. The passes through them give one some fine peeps either over the plains or across through the mountain valleys; there are waterfalls and torrents and great pools of crystal-clear water; the paths wander up and down the mountains, sometimes with one side sheer precipice, through cool shaded forest out into the broiling sunshine of a grassy patch, and back once more into the dark shelter of gigantic trees.

The district of Krachi is always good to look at, with its mountains and its many watercourses. Other districts depend for their attractiveness on the weather, which we discuss quite as much out here as at home, for, contrary to general belief, our weather is far from being constant.

On the coast the influence of the sea is felt, and naturally in the rain-forest, which is not far inland, stretching less than two hundred miles inland, that influence is still felt to a certain extent, but the vital factor in the weather on the Gold Coast is the strength of the trade-winds. Actually the whole country lies within the area of the north-east trade, but owing to a bend northward of the zone, of low barometric pressure, the south-east trade crosses the Equator and, obedient to the law which governs winds, is deflected and becomes a south-west monsoon. This monsoon is the prevalent wind on the coast.

The area of low pressure more or less coincides with the rain-forest, so that both the south-west monsoon and the north-east trade meet there, with the inevitable result of heavy rains and, not unusually, strong winds. The monsoon is the stronger in the rain-forest, and extends during three months—July, August, September—to the north as far as the fourteenth parallel, but for the rest of the year the trade prevails and reverses the process in the rain-forest, where it triumphs over the monsoon for about the same period of three months—December, January, February.

This eternal combat between the monsoon and the trade explains what at first seems extraordinary—namely, that in the north our rain almost invariably comes from the east or north-east, and that in that quarter every storm or tornado will arise. What actually happens is that the colder and drier north-east comes into contact with the hotter and saturated monsoon. The advance of the trade is marked by the precipitation of the monsoon's dampness, and naturally causes great inrushes of air.

It is most interesting I think to watch this phenomenon, and one can with considerable accuracy forecast a tornado by merely watching the layers of cloud. One often witnesses the actual beginning of these violent cyclonic storms, and on my last tour from my house at Krachi I could watch not only the commencement of the storm but follow for miles its course, and now and then even see its finish. The absence of the necessary instruments prevents one from making observations of value.

These tornadoes are sometimes of terrific force and somewhat terrifying. Usually they occur in the afternoon or evening, but not always, and during May they are quite regular at about nine A.M. in the extreme north. They are heralded by intense heat and brightness, due to the presence of the monsoon's air, which is damp. Later, one will notice the clouds passing from the south-west at a lesser speed than earlier, whilst an upper layer, slower in the morning, is now hasting south-west. In the north-eastern quarter clouds will be gathering into great cumuli; gradually this cumulus will reach up to the zenith and spread itself, until it forms a dense cloud-mass all over that quarter. By this time the north-east wind is asserting itself and the cloud-mass begins to race forward. At this juncture the clouds are driven along in layers by the oncoming trade, which evidently varies in force at different levels.

These layers assume the shape of an arc, which gradually becomes better and better defined until it stands out as a fearsome black bow across the heavens. All this time there has been plenty of lightning, which now concentrates itself behind the arc, the edge of which marks the beginning of the rain.

As the arc advances over the zenith there comes that two-minute calm so often talked of, but one can hear the roar of the approaching wind and the noise of the rain smashing on to the leaves and ground. A gust or two of terrific violence, and the tornado itself is on one. In a few seconds the rain arrives; the gale ceases to increase, as a rule, though it will retain its first force for some time. Gradually the wind expends itself, and in a comparatively short time rain and storm will have passed away. The track is marked by unroofed houses, broken trees, and so on, and after heavy rain there will be the lines of newly made waterways. But rain does not always come in these tornadoes: in the far north the first tornadoes of the season are nearly always dust-storms, more awe-inspiring than the rain ones, for the lightning seems so much more fearsome when no rain comes with it. The lightning gives a beautiful display at times, pink and bluish, but the continuous thunder is a trifle worrying.

Sometimes hail will accompany a tornado. Five times have I witnessed that phenomenon out here, and the last time it was terrifying. The stones fell at the beginning of the tornado and were then the size of an ordinary dried pea; they gradually grew larger and became square-shaped, but with jagged ends, and were quite the size of an ordinary lump of sugar; their size increased until they were of an incredible size. These last ones were flower-shaped, with the petals deflected and the centre of the flower somewhat flattened. They must have acquired that shape in a cyclone of cyclones. They were so large that the centre covered a two-shilling piece, and the petals stretched out so that one could not arrange two of them without overlapping on an ordinary envelope. This downpour lasted for just over twenty minutes, and left the whole place covered—possibly six inches deep—with the stones, which had not melted three-quarters of an hour later. The people came out of their huts in crowds, and collected basketfuls and calabashfuls of the hailstones. These they ate. The children especially were fond of them. Next morning many repented.

The downfall was very local, and did not stretch in width for much more than a mile, for on the following day one could trace its extent easily enough, since the stones had at the beginning been driven as much as two inches into the ground, which was left, when the ice melted, all pock-marked. No one went out during this phenomenon, naturally, and I don't think many were caught in it either. But just when it was over I talked to a man who had evidently been out in it. I asked him: "Were you in this storm?" He said: "Yes, I was on the river fishing." I then said: "Did the stones hurt you?" "Hurt! Master," he replied very quietly, "those stones have nearly killed me. I could not bear them in my canoe so I jumped into the water, and every time my head came up those stones drove me under." To me the marvel was that he was not killed. He was a very scared man.

In the Krachi district fishing is, as one might expect, a very important industry. The rivers are many and wide, and have innumerable good fishing-places. The local people, however, are but poor fishermen, and the industry is almost entirely in the hands of some natives from near the coast, whom the Krachi group—wrongly—under one name, Bator, that being one of their villages.

Their fishing is remarkably efficient, and large catches are made, the fish being smoked and dried on the banks, or on islands in the rivers, to be sold later in the coast markets. The method of catching the fish is both interest-

RETURNING FROM THE RIVER.

Konkomba youths with fishing nets on their way home after an afternoon's 'company' fishing.

COMPANY FISHING (2 and 3).

In all parts of the country north of the Forest the people fish ponds and pools in this fashion. There is much jollification, and good catches are made.

ing and instructive to watch. The Bators come up the river in gangs or families, and settle on some sandbank, or other such place. There they erect temporary shelters of bamboo and reeds and grass, for themselves and their womenfolk, who usually accompany them; and there they have their headquarters for the season. The local natives have rights over their waters and the invading Bators pay rent each season at so much per canoe.

Fishing takes place at all times of the day, and is regulated by the head man of the party. About a baker's dozen of canoes take part, each manned by two youths, a paddle-man and a netman. The canoes proceed in a line across the river, and when the reach which is to be fished is arrived at, the centre halts and both wings advance, converging, so that at one time a formation of a **V** is made. The canoes at the top then turn towards each other and, at a given signal, each netman casts his net in such a manner as to encircle almost completely the water round the canoes. Great skill is shown in handling the nets, which are of a very fine mesh and heavily leaded.

Local fishers are far less skilled, and their clumsier casts naturally produce smaller catches. From long contact with Europeans they prefer line and hook, and lay night-lines at many places. All along the banks one sees little platforms, obviously erected for fishers. I asked why, and was told "the crocodiles won't catch you unawares"!

But the favourite method of capturing fish is by the use of a narcotic. This is produced from a plant, *Trephosia vogelii*, which is cultivated throughout all the open country north of the rain-forest. The leaves are crushed and moulded with mud into balls, which are freshly prepared each time. Fishing takes place not in the river, but in the ponds and pools and meres which line the banks of most rivers.

At the date agreed upon, men, women and children flock to the pool. They carry nets and baskets and bags and gourds. Arrived on the ground, a sacrifice to the spirit of the water is made, and numbers of the *Trephosia* balls are thrown into the pond, which in a few minutes becomes inky black. After about ten minutes the fish begin to come up to the surface, and at once the water is invaded by the people, who seize the temporarily asphyxiated fish.

This would seem a very wasteful method of fish-taking, and one would imagine that fish would soon cease to be found in these waters. However, such is not the case. There are innumerable laws, broken, as in England, chiefly by children, to govern fishing. There are recognized seasons for certain fish, which the elders report are poisonous at other times; waters are often preserved for a number of years; and certain methods of capture are forbidden. They are all native laws, and are very generally observed by the local people. Strangers are less meticulous.

Taking fish in common is practised throughout the Northern Protectorate, and frequently without the use of the asphyxiating plant. One can imagine the excitement and fun of catching fish all alive-o! in the hand or basket or net, with everyone shouting and playing about.

There are fifteen hundred recognized species of fish in West African fresh waters, but who can tell how many that are still unknown to science? They vary from the most minute to the giant Niger perch, found frequently in the waters of the Volta, which will attain a weight of two hundred pounds and more. Some are excellent to eat, some are poisonous, and most are too bony. Several varieties of fish capable of giving electric shocks are to be found; but one must always beware of handling these tropical fish, for they frequently give nasty cuts with the spines on their backs or fins, or even tails, and more often than not such cuts will be poisonous.

The most curious fish, to my mind, are those dug up out of the ground during the dry season. There are two sorts of these that I have come across. One variety apparently lives in pools which dry up towards the end of the season, leaving a smooth, baked-clay surface. This the people hoe up, and collect an evil-smelling dark-green fish, about five inches long. The other variety is found on land which at the height of maximum flood is covered with water. This fish lives singly, and only in the Konkomba country have I seen it.

One day I was trying to cut across country in a direction more or less parallel to the River Monyoch. The route lay across a grassy plain which was, during the rains, at times flooded, but which was then broken up into cakes of very hard mud, so hard that it reminded me irresistibly of frozen land. My guide went off whilst we were resting, and proceeded to dig with his axe—a sort of tool capable of many uses, and as indispensable to a Konkomba as the knife proverbially is to a sailor. I inquired what he was digging for, and was told fish. And he found it too, about a foot below the surface in clay.

I asked how he knew it was there, but the explanation not being sufficiently clear he said he would show me. He did so some little time afterwards, and pointing to a sod said that a fish was there. I could see nothing to indicate this. However, the fish was there, and we were at least half-a-mile from the river, nor had water lain there for at least three months. I know of no explanation for this peculiarity of the fish.

Fish are rather more carefully preserved by native customary law than are the wild animals, which are hunted by the villagers in company, just as are the water "meat." The rules are laid down quite clearly, and are maintained by religious fear, which is after all the greatest moulder of public opinion. For who dare offend a law if to his offence will be attributed any evil that may befall his neighbour? Fishing-time is settled by the elders, or sometimes by the owner of the pond, just as hunting-time is. The latter in the south is arranged for at that period when fire will most thoroughly consume the grass. That is, undoubtedly, the result of a close study of "fly," for at that period most larvæ are destroyed, together with the undergrowth. In the north there is a curious custom observed before setting fire to the grass.

There is a large lizard usually met with close to the habitation of man. It is blue-grey, with a vermilion head and a vermilion tail. All sorts of magical attributes are believed to reside in the body of this rather awesome beast, possibly owing to its association with houses. Particularly is this so where fire is concerned, and, when all the omens point to a favourable occasion for setting the bush afire, one is caught and to its body is attached a brand. It is released on a path in the selected area, and whichever way it turns that path is burned, and the torches necessary are taken from the grass the lizard has set alight.

But to return to fish. Practically everywhere one will find preserves of fish. There is the almost classic example of the Tano river in Ashanti. That river is the abode of a most powerful spirit, and everything in contact with it is sacred. Fish, therefore, are sacred, and by no man at all may they be molested if they are in the sacred waters. But whenever the river is swollen, overflows, banks up the inflowing streams, fish may be taken, provided they are not on the dry-season bosom of the water. A very sound rule, since fish are thereby completely protected for six months at least, and partially so for the remainder of the year.

The fish seem to have realized this immunity, and one can witness at any crossing of the river some rather interesting sights. For instance, I have stood in the river itself and have had the water all around me swarming with fish. They actually touched my legs. This lack of shyness is due to the custom observed by almost every-one of feeding them whenever they cross or approach the river. That custom is actually compulsory on natives of the country.

But stranger than that was to watch the fish answering a call. At the Tano river ford close to a village called Acherensua there was—probably still is—a path leading a little downstream. It took me to a clearing overhanging the river, where sacrifices were made to the Great Spirit of the Tano. If one asked the village priest he would proceed to this spot and ring a bell, a native one of brass, shaped rather like the cow-bells of the Schwarzwald. Almost at once the water was broken by the fish coming to the noise, until the river seemed to be a seething mass of large and small fish, which we fed.

In most other places one will find similar religious restrictions which tend to conserve the fish. But there is also another reason for this protection. The illogical reasoning which is so general among these people, of "*post hoc, propter hoc,*" attributes the presence of water to fish being in it: "If you catch the fish, the water will fail us"—an argument which accounts in many cases for protection afforded to crocodiles.

Such protection of fish is afforded at Nangodi, in the Zuaragu district, and at Nyambo, in the Krachi district. At the former place the pool is a large one and contains innumerable fish, which may be caught in the outlet but not in the pond itself. At Nyambo the fish are very small, smaller than minnows. They live in a little water-hole in the bed of a stream, which dries up during the dry season and leaves only a few puddles. In one such stream under an overhanging rock lies this sacred pool. One can easily catch the fish, and boys do this, but they always replace them and feed them.

One is struck by the kindness and consideration with which fish are thus treated, until one remembers that to the native all things have a soul, with human attributes. They dig up the stone that has caused one to stumble and, throwing it away, remark: "O stone! you can rest in the bush and no longer hurt the feet of men." They address the thorn that has torn them, while breaking it: " O thorn! you have hurt me. I break you and never more shall you hurt a man."

But the most striking incident of that sort was in Ashanti. I was out one evening with a couple of Ashanti youths and a gun. One of the boys called my attention to the whistling of some kob, and I decided to go and try for a shot. So leaving them I went ahead and, getting within easy range, dropped the buck, a fine beast.

The boys came up, and at once began to cut up the meat, whilst all the time one of them addressed himself somewhat as follows to the dead animal: " O kob! you were the Chief of Kobs, and now you are dead. You were a proud kob, but now you are dead. Three times have I hunted you, and three times I have missed. O kob! you were too proud to die from a black man's gun. But the white man has killed you. O Kob! to-night you will rest in my belly." The boy was pleased with his words, and began to sing them, whilst his comrade joined in a chorus of " Now you are dead " after each sentence.

CHAPTER VIII

BIG-GAME HUNTING

THE most fascinating of pastimes, I think, is that of big-game shooting or stalking. Not only does one enjoy the zest of hunting, but one also has the infinite pleasure of being out in the wild, and of innumerable opportunities of watching the apparent wonders of nature.

Big-game shooting—or as we call it locally " hunting " —on the Gold Coast is not to be compared with the same sport in East or South Africa. The Gold Coast, even with its two dependencies, is only a small country, and there is neither the quantity of game nor the variety. However, good sport can be obtained in most districts except those on the coast, which generally are to all intents gameless.

There are two distinct types of hunting, that of the forest and that of the Sudan zone. The former is very difficult for a European, who cannot expect large bags, but can be assured of a magnificent opportunity of studying and watching a little-known corner of nature. Owing to the character of the forest country it is not usual for a European to hunt therein alone. He must accompany native hunters.

Never shall I forget my days in the forest zone, when I was able to snatch the time to go with my villagers. It was not possible to arrange on the previous night a hunt

THE BOWL OF FRIENDSHIP.

Two Konkomba youths at Sambul market drinking millet beer from one gourd as a sign of their great friendship.

for the following day: one had to give a few days' notice, so that the terrain could be discussed, the deities propitiated, and so forth. In West Africa one is for ever being impressed with the truth that haste is useless, and best results are obtained after due consideration and thorough deliberation.

Once the day for the hunt was settled, preparations began in earnest. The flint-lock guns—which we call Dane guns, presumably because they were first introduced by the Danish merchants, who long were established on the coast—were cleaned; powder was obtained; favourite bullets, either of lead or stone, which are used often over and over again, were got out of some secret hiding-place; powder belts and horns were overhauled; old pieces of cloth prepared for wads. All this was carried out without fuss, for the natives are in such matters not given to show excitement, but remain very serious and deliberate.

At last my first hunting day with them came. The rendezvous was the village assembly tree before dawn. I was first to arrive, but that, I think, was arranged on purpose, either to prove to me that hunting was really an everyday affair, or out of courtesy to one whom they considered their superior. But I was not kept waiting. As soon as ever I had reached the tree the elder men came out, and we soon mustered some forty-three guns, and a number of youths and boys unarmed.

Everyone except the boys was garbed in old discoloured and torn clothes; those with guns had leather pouch-belts, and most wore leather necklaces holding charms, or strange rope or leather armlets and bracelets, favourite mascots to bring luck or to avert catastrophe. There was not much talking—that had been done before. Presently the chief of the village brought up to me a middle-aged man who was the leader of the hunt. After a few words of greeting he asked me if I were ready, and on receiving my answer marched down the path leading from the village. We followed in single file, and entered into the blue mist which hung around the trees of the uncleared forest, for the sun was not yet above the horizon. After about an hour's march we came to a little path leading out of the main one, and our leader halted. When all had come up the head hunter gave some rapid instructions, and half the number of armed men, and all the unarmed ones, marched off down the main path.

We sat down and smoked. Conversation was not very general, no one seeming to have much to say. After a half-hour's wait our leader arose, and we filed silently down a little, almost unnoticeable, path, right into the heart of the forest.

Often one hears that the Ashanti forest is a great impenetrable jungle, with an undergrowth so riotously luxuriant that it is not possible to pass. This is absolutely false. Once one leaves paths where sunlight can penetrate, and thereby enable the shorter plant-life to thrive, one enters into a dark, sunless region, with very few creepers or lianas on the trees, which reach branchless for even two hundred feet above one, at which height they are crowned with a thick crest of verdure through which the sunshine cannot pierce. One can see for almost a hundred yards, and in places even farther. In the early morning it is quite pleasantly cool, but ceaseless drops of moisture from above make everything very damp.

After proceeding for some twenty minutes in this dim light we seemed to come to an end of the path, but the leader continued for a while. No one was talking, and our feet made no noise, for the ground was too damp to allow even twigs to crack beneath the pressure of bare feet. Only my boots now and then betrayed our march. When the path had, so far as I could see, completely disappeared the leader detailed off hunters to stop every fifty yards or so, taking the precaution to station the two most experienced on either side of me. They were well in view then, but very soon after had completely screened themselves behind trees, or on the ground, so that except for my orderly I seemed to be quite alone in the forest.

There was a complete silence, for though the forest teems with life in reality, every moving beast, even insects, seemed to be aware of our presence, and had hidden themselves noiselessly away. In eager expectancy for the unknown I waited. Nearly an hour passed, and then one could hear a distant noise of drumming, which grew clearer and clearer, till whistling and shouting also could be distinguished. Now and then, far away, a gun had been fired, not in our line but from among the advancing beaters.

Then came a sudden change in the forest. Nothing had been visible in front of me save the motionless tree-trunks; but now dull-coloured forms moving along the leaf-covered ground could be made out. Mice, squirrels and small birds came first. Later larger animals, francolins and crested blue guinea-fowl scurried along. The beaters drew nearer; the drumming, shouting and whistling grew louder and louder, till the whole forest became a pandemonium of noise. Frequently guns were fired, both on my flanks and in front. I saw a large animal not far from where I knew lay hid my left-hand neighbour. He fired. There was a howl and a scurry. Men seemed suddenly to take shape out of the dimness. The hunt was over. In a very short time all came together, some empty-handed, others with a dead duiker and one or two with the foot of an animal too large for one man to carry. This last was to prove that he had slain the beast, for, here as elsewhere, seeing is the only form of believing in the hunting-field. As for the man who had fired on my left and hit something, he was searching the ground very carefully for marks.

Presently he shouted, and two or three men went towards where he had gone into a thicket. There was a shot, and after a while the men came back carrying with them a large serval cat. Curiously enough, it was the same cat that had been robbing my hen-roost, and which I had shot in the hindquarters three weeks previously. My pellets had not broken any bones, but were found just under the skin.

The bag was indeed a varied one: two yellow-backed duikers, five blue duikers, two squirrels of a very large size, one blue crested guinea-fowl and a francolin. It was an unusually large kill. We carried out, however, two more drives.

This forest-hunting in company is very exciting. The noise of the drivers, the shouting and firing, animals and men dimly visible, all tend to make one reckless, and accidents are common. I attended the hunts quite often, and myself, fortunately, never witnessed a mishap, though I have had to deal in court with a good many.

Hunting alone in the forest is practically impossible for a European. Not only would he find it difficult not to be lost, but he cannot glide as silently as the native, nor as a rule has he their power of remaining motionless for hours on one of the paths which the animals make, and along which they travel regularly. Moreover, it requires a long experience to train one's eye to make out an animal in the dim light of the forest.

It is interesting to record, what I think is the fact, that our eyes usually detect a moving animal before the native, and that he looks for their legs whilst we look for their heads.

Native hunters—I talk of the Ashanti—will go several days into the forest. They take a quantity of food with them—enough, with the meat obtained, to keep them for a week or so. Usually they go in pairs, and they lie in wait on the path, or sometimes will call the "meat" (we call all animals of the bush or forest "meat" or "beef").

This method is very curious, and at the same time very successful. The hunter conceals himself and then emits a deep call, keeping his mouth open and patting it frequently with one hand. All kinds of animals will come to see what the noise is, and I myself have seen a blue duiker answer the call. Once a very fine leopard was brought to me; it had been called up by its slayer. I gave Kojo a tin trumpet when he was still a child. He said it would be excellent for "calling meat," and sent it to an uncle who used it successfully.

In the Ashanti forest there are to be found elephant,

buffalo, two kinds of pig, bongo, bush-buck, and to my knowledge eight, therefore there must be more, different species of duiker, ranging in size from the yellow-backed duiker, which is as large as a Sicilian donkey, to the royal duiker, as small as a shipperke. Leopards, servals, civets and other cats are numerous, but very difficult to see. They like to wander at night, or when the sun is hottest, for at these hours they alone are afoot. Of game-birds in the forest there are francolins, the blue guinea-fowl, the green pigeon, several other species of pigeon and two sorts of bush-fowl.

Natives, of course, do a considerable amount of trapping, but with indifferent success. The ingenious noose-trap, which seems fairly general throughout Africa, is used for duikers of the smaller variety, fall-traps for squirrels and rats are often seen by the sides of the paths. But in the forest I saw no traps of outstanding character save one, which Kojo used to supply me regularly with a francolin, locally called *Aboko*. This is a small bird, but very plump, and makes excellent eating. The method of capture was as follows.

Kojo cleared a bare space at the side of the path in the real forest, as distinct from the jungle, till it resembled a dusting-place. For two or three days he ground-baited the spot with a few grains of corn. He then erected two sticks about eighteen inches high and about fifteen inches apart. He tied cross-sticks, one at the top and one at the bottom, and then wove string up and down between these bars, until the trap looked rather like a small loom. He then put some grains on one side only. Now the curious part of this arrangement was that the francolin could have taken without any risk the whole of the grains, but for some reason or other the bird preferred to put its head through the strings, which had been smeared with raw rubber, and thus it was held fast till the boy returned. I was very fond of *Aboko*, and never failed to have a brace whenever I told Kojo to go and get them.

Other birds caught by boys are chiefly canaries and parrots. The canaries are caught in birdcages, wherein one is already a prisoner and acts as a decoy. The wild ones enter different compartments, of which the doors close in answer to a spring. This, however, I am sure, was an introduction by the Germans, who carried on a large trade in feathered captives. It is interesting to note that these birds are well looked after, and more than well fed, by the children, who carry them about wherever they go.

The parrots usually caught are the grey ones, which often make such good talkers. But unfortunately the usual method of capture is very cruel. These birds fly, as a rule, in large flocks, and often come down in the evening to a mud-bank near the rivers. The boys note this and ground-bait the place. Then one day they strew it with raw rubber as well as grain, and several of the birds are unable to fly off, thereby being easily taken by the children, who to rid the bird of the rubber have to pluck out the feathers. Some parrots are almost entirely plucked before they are free, and often die of shock. The survivors are caged and fed up until new feathers are grown, and the birds are sufficiently decent-looking to be sold.

This plucking alive is quite common, and, until one

has quite impressed one's intense dislike to the practice, obtains both in the kitchen and on the shooting-field. There is no implied deliberate cruelty in this, merely thoughtlessness.

Traps constructed on the principle of the cage mouse-traps at home are built for leopards, hyenas and larger cats by the Ashantis on the northern outskirts of the forest, and extend throughout the country inland. They are made of mud and completely covered up. At the extreme end is tied a goat or lamb, which is attached to a cord that goes over the trap and holds in place a wooden door. The leopard enters, seizes the bait, and thereby releases the door, which falls behind and closes the exit. It is then shot, holes having been left sufficiently large for a Dane gun at the height where a mortal shot might be expected.

When I was at Sunyanî a tragedy occurred at Odumase over a leopard trapped and shot in this way. The trap had not been made sufficiently narrow, so that the leopard had room to turn round. He was wounded in the hind-quarters, and when the trap was opened slew two men and one woman, and mauled several others of the crowd which had gathered. It was a very large specimen, measuring nine feet two inches from tip to tail, but was not in good condition, its fur being thin and mangy.

Of all the animals in the forest, pride of place must be given, I think, to the bongo. This is a very large antelope, of the same family as the bush-buck or harnessed antelope. Of a rufous brown, its flanks and spine are strikingly marked with white lines. Its horns, smooth and slightly twisted, have white tips and run to—the largest I have seen—as much as thirty-nine inches. The females also are horned. It is said that no European has ever killed one on the Gold Coast, but there is a record in the game-book of the Gold Coast Regiment of an eland having been slain at Kintampo. As elands are not found on the Gold Coast it is more than likely that a bongo is meant, although there is a possibility that an eland did wander so far, for they are found to the north and west.

The bongo is an animal which enjoys a certain reputation among the Ashanti. Not everyone will kill them, as they are "too strong a medicine." At Goaso I wanted some heads to decorate the station and to act as a guide as to what animals there were in the forest, for it is commonly alleged that there is no game. I got specimens of most and then asked for a bongo. In the course of a month five were brought me. The carriers came stark naked: ankles, knees, wrists, arms and neck had bound on them bracelets of some herbs. I was told that evil was thereby avoided, as the bongo was a very powerful animal and possessed much magic.

I have hunted bongo several times, and once came on spoor less than a quarter of an hour old. The nearest I ever came to one was when out company-hunting, when one hunter killed a young one about two hundred yards off. All the natives laugh when one tells them that white men have never killed one of these animals. They say that it is the easiest animal of all to hunt. They are usually in groups of four or five, and even as many as twelve. They feed both in the thicker forest and on the outskirts, where the cultivated fields are of new elephant-grass, but are particularly fond of the leaves of an arum-lily. At dawn, at midday and at dusk are the best times to hunt them, for it is then they feed. They are not shy and will not make off even after a shot has been fired. They are fond of keeping on the same run, which always includes a good salt-lick. It is only because of their "magic," which inspires respect, that they have not been exterminated, for very few men will dare to kill more than three, and few dare kill any.

The bongo area stretches into the grass country as far as the forest has left thickets, but where these cease —that is to say, where they are no longer of any extent— the bongo is not to be found at all.

But before writing about hunting in the open country it is worth, I think, making mention of a very curious trap set by Nature. In some of the clearings in the forest where man has long ceased to go there is now and then to be found a grass, known to us as devil-grass. Its seeds are covered with a very strong glue, with which the tops of the grass are all matted together. I first came across this in very painful circumstances. I was walking along a little-used path when I suddenly felt what seemed like a red-hot iron searing my knee. The grass had caught the hair on it, and, not knowing then what it was, I had my other knee caught at once. It was only with the aid of a native who was with me that I could release myself without considerable pain. It is said that small animals are very frequently caught and held by this grass. The more they struggle the more they are entangled, and cannot get released save by death.

Hunting in the open country can be had sixty miles north of Coomassie and onward. It is very different to the forest work, and one can (and always does) hunt alone, save for one's guide, and maybe the orderly as well. It is hard work, and most kills have been well earned. The country presents a park-like or orchard appearance, with increasingly large tracks of treeless land the farther one proceeds north. One's range of vision is correspondingly greater and the animals are far easier to detect. During August, and right on to January or February, hunting is impossible, as the grass is too high, reaching sometimes to seven or eight feet. But soon after the New Year the whole country is burnt and one can wander about freely, though what with the dust from the ashes and the wind-brought dust from the Sahara it is not very pleasant tramping. In March, however, a few showers fall, and by April the grass is generally everywhere sprouting, and the country becomes beautiful to look at, easy to cover and not difficult to hunt over. May and June are by far the best months, as the growth of plants is by then general.

In this Sudanese zone the variety of animals is far greater. We have elephant, lion, leopard, hyena, serval, civet and other cats, buffalo, roan, hartebeest (two species), water-buck, kob, bush-buck, reed-buck, oribi, several duiker, wart-hog, two other kinds of pig, wild dog and, in the extreme north only, a gazelle. In bird-life there are two or three kinds of partridge, guinea-fowl, many species of pigeon, snipe, two or three species of duck, quail, plover, sand-grouse and teal. One can see that in the Protectorate there is plenty of variety in shooting, and to one who cares for the sport a very fascinating opportunity for exercise and change.

Pride of place must be given, in my opinion, to buffalo-hunting. Often one is asked which is the most dangerous of animals to hunt, and various answers are given—some hunters say lion, others elephant, others rhinoceros, others buffalo. In the Gold Coast hinterland there are no rhinoceroses; lions are not numerous; elephant-hunting cannot be indulged in to any extent, nor are they looked on by the natives as—apart from their "magic"—dangerous; but every native agrees that buffalo are bad, and my experience will agree with that opinion. Moreover, buffalo are fairly common in most districts, whereas lion and elephant afford only occasional opportunities.

CHAPTER IX

LIONS, LEOPARDS & ELEPHANTS

BUT lion-killing is, I think, the aim of most of us. Probably this is a remnant of boyish ambition. Lions, in spite of the fact that one often sees in print that there are no lions on the Gold Coast, are to be found as far south as the forest belt; but they are far more common north of the ninth parallel.

My first lion came to me by accident. I was in the Kanjaga or, more properly, Bura country, and had finished hunting for the day. My path to the rest-house lay along a stream, which had steep banks, and was about thirty feet wide. My orderly suddenly called my attention to a large "meat" on the other bank. It was standing close against some tall brown grass on an ash-covered clearing. There was a thick haze hovering about the ground, and though clear for about five feet it was fairly thick above that. The effect was strange, and I saw what seemed an enormous animal. I asked the man what it was, and he answered: "Pig." The target, in spite of the mirage, was a good one, and I fired. I heard the bullet tell, and as the animal went into the grass saw its tail. That completely fogged me. It certainly, to my mind, was not a pig's. However, the orderly was so insistent, and he had done so much hunting, that I began to believe him, and when we had crossed the stream he took me straight to the spot where a pig had been rooting. This convinced me, and telling him to follow the spoor I myself circled round and entered the grass. This stretched only a few yards, and as I emerged into the open there also issued out, about five yards only from me, a lioness. I fired, and she gave a growl, but it was her last, as she rolled over at once, dead. Just at that moment a wart-hog galloped away. I had not seen it, whereas the orderly had not seen my lioness.

Another lion hunt was not so successful. A male lion had become a terrible nuisance in my district and that of my neighbour. He had already accounted for twenty-three human victims before I had the time to spare to hunt him. When I reached the area he was preying upon I found a state almost of terror. Men armed with bows and arrows accompanied the womenfolk when the latter went to the watering-place; work in the field was restricted to those fields close to the houses. A small boy had been watching the millet to drive away the birds, and as usual he was stationed on a raised platform. Presently he saw a large animal and he fired three arrows at it, raising at the same time as a warning the war-cry. He knew the animal had been hit but had not been killed. Therefore he had to remain on his platform, and it was some hours before he ventured to climb down and run home. Meanwhile everyone had hurried back, and the men, fully armed, turned out, but naturally did not enter the standing corn, as they could neither see nor shoot any beast that might be lurking therein. When they met the boy and learned that the lion had been wounded, for three days none dared go forth. Then the chief organized a battue, and they discovered near the field the dead body of a leopard. It must be remembered that the houses are not close together, but are detached, and surrounded by fields for some distance, so that to walk from one to the other was a perilous adventure, since the paths are very narrow between the standing guinea-corn or millet, that reaches from ten to fifteen feet in height. Communication in these circumstances can be carried out only by shouting or whistling.

Meanwhile the lion had accounted for more victims, and I had arrived on the scene. The movements of the lion had been fairly regular. He had been hunting in an area of about ten miles on either side of a twenty-mile stretch of the Sissili river. He would kill two or three times on consecutive days and would then lie up for a week, to reappear about five miles downstream, returning on his tracks when he had reached the southernmost limit of his self-appointed run.

We expected to come up with him near the settlement known as Wiasi. On the evening of the second day after my arrival an old hunter came to me and reported that he knew where the lion watered, and that if I made an early start I might be in time to catch him. Therefore before dawn I set out through the fields which stretched down to the banks of the Sissili. When we reached that river, which was nearly dry, we went upstream and came to a good pool. This was the lion's watering-place, but he had either winded us or had finished drinking, for we saw only his tracks, with the mud still freshly stirred up in his pad-marks. He had not crossed but had returned to the other bank, away from the river across open country, apparently to some rock-strewn hills. It was not possible to follow him as the earth was too dry to show any tracks, so I decided to give up hunting him that morning and turned upstream. The country was quite open and covered with new grass, looking not unlike meadowland without hedges. Close to the river there were clusters of tall brown grass which had escaped the annual burning, with small valleys into which the river flooded during the rains. To my surprise I came across a reed-buck in one of these little nullahs, and I shot it. Leaving the animal, I turned towards where I had noticed three young men, armed with bows and arrows, standing on the cliff-bank of the river. When we came close to them, being separated only by a valley which was bare, and a ridge of tall unburned grass on the opposite side, where the young men were—the whole distance being less than seventy-five yards—I told them to bring the "meat" along. Scarcely had I spoken than out of the grass leapt the lion. It passed me at a terrific speed, and in my state of surprise I missed him. There is no doubt but that he was actually stalking the youths.

That lion left the district and moved some fifty miles westward, where, after claiming two more victims, he was killed in a general battue.

Man-eaters are not usual, however; but it seems that the truce in hunting caused by the war encouraged them. There were two of them six miles to the north of my bungalow at Navaro. They roamed over a very small area just across the frontier, in French territory, but on land cultivated by our people. They killed twelve people before being exterminated.

IN BIMBA MARKET.

These markets are more social than commercial, for all are protected from attack going or coming by the Spirit of the Market.

CLEANING FIBRE.

The fibre is cleaned by women and made into string by men by rubbing and rolling it against the thigh.

Another man-eater passed through my district. He left a grim token of his passage on one of the paths leading from the Nankanni country into the Bura—two hands and two feet. They belonged to a Bura man, whose brother swore revenge on all lions. His opportunity came some three months later. Two lions leapt over the wall of a hut in Fambissi where some cattle were shut up in the yard for the night. They killed one and the rest of the herd stampeded, breaking down the gate. The lions followed and slew two more, but the men in the hut-compound—there were only two of them—had been aroused by the noise and had followed the herd in the moonlight, which, the moon happening to be at the full, was almost as clear as daylight. They came up with the lions on their kill and fired their arrows at them. One of the lions was hit and it turned on the nearer man, whom it killed. Meanwhile the other man had climbed a tree, and he fired, and again succeeded in hitting the wounded lion, which leapt up the tree and knocked him out. By this time more people had arrived on the scene, and the lions made off without killing the second man, who was able to tell the tale. But he died three days later.

The countryside was roused and scores of men turned out to hunt the lions. The news reached the brother who had sworn his vendetta, and he hurried to the place. That same day the lions were cornered, and he marched up against them singing, or rather shouting, an impromptu song of defiance and revenge. Apparently everyone watched. It was rather difficult to learn the exact details at the subsequent inquest, but it would seem that the man advanced, calling on his dead brother's soul to help, and to see how he would be revenged. He went straight against the male, the originally wounded one, which was standing roaring, and when he was well within range he fired, and the arrow pierced the lion's heart—a wonderful shot considering the shortness of the arrow, which is only about eighteen inches long. The lioness, which had been crouching and watching the man, leapt straight at him. He fired and hit her, but she killed him, and standing over the corpse roared her defiance to the crowd of watchers, who closed on her from all sides, and finished her off with scores of arrows.

The above story is rather curious, as it shows how angry the villagers must have been. Usually lions are left alone and driven off their kill of cattle by sticks and stones—almost incredible; and it is only when the people are thoroughly aroused that they attempt to kill them. An ex-soldier living at a place called Katigri had a horse. A lion killed it. He asked his relations to help him kill the lion, but they refused, and he, being the only angered person, went out and succeeded in obtaining his revenge.

This custom, arising, I suppose, out of the principle of letting sleeping dogs lie, is sometimes rather annoying. I had been after lion in the Bachawnsi Hills, a wild rock-strewn country with some fairly lofty kopjes. All the morning I had heard them roaring, but was unable to come up with them. At nine o'clock I reached the rest-house, and had scarcely begun to change when a runner came in saying that two lions had just killed a couple of cows not fifteen minutes away, near where I had lately passed. I had seen the herd of cattle, and had expressed the view that it seemed rather to be asking for trouble to send them out to pasture just where the lions were. However, I was told that the lions never kill the Bachawnsi cows—a stupid remark, and one crying aloud for contradiction, especially as it is precisely one of those boasting remarks which natives and farmers all the world over abhor.

I dressed and went out. There were the two dead cows, but the lions had been driven off and, of course, would not be seen again that day.

The first lion I ever saw in the wild was in the Yendi country. I had gone out to shoot a kob for the pot. It was in December and the grass had not been burnt, therefore it was very high. But the natives had burnt a few small spaces in order to allow some new grass to sprout before the rains ceased altogether, thus enabling their cattle to remain in better condition than those who would have to depend a month more on the dried-up grass. These spaces were used as feeding-ground also by herds of kob, which, owing to the smallness of the patches, were difficult to approach.

As we came near the spot chosen, the guide climbed a tree to obtain a view. I leant against the tree and waited with my orderly. Presently the man up the tree became very excited and, without speaking, made gestures that an animal was lying apparently at the foot of a tree not five yards from us. A native's pointing is so ill-aimed, as a rule, that it is practically useless. However this time the man evidently was trying to indicate that the animal was very close. I could see nothing, but after a while made out some village cows coming through the grass. Then the herd stampeded, and I had a fine view of a lion in mid-air. It had evidently winded me and leapt away, fortunately from me and from the cattle.

Of the other cats one rarely catches a glimpse. I have seen three leopards together—a family party—but they were out of range and were moving rapidly. On another occasion I had a fine view of one standing on a rock and presenting an easy mark. I missed it.

Once my hunter got very excited over a leopard which, he said, was drinking at a pool in the river. I was within twenty-five yards of the pool but could see nothing. It moved off still without my viewing it, and all I saw were its tracks.

The only serval I have seen was the one in the forest zone, already mentioned; and the sole civet I ever saw I spared, as he was too easy a shot and too beautiful to kill. The natives frequently bring in to us the kittens of these latter. They make good pets, but when older become difficult to handle.

Elephants are, after lion, the most sought-for prize. This is really a great pity, and will presumably lead to their eventual extinction in this part of the world. It is practically impossible to preserve them, and as their meat alone is worth from twenty-five to fifty pounds, according to size, only the most drastic punishments would deter a hunter from slaying them.

A few years ago, when first the white man penetrated the interior, elephants were certainly very much more numerous. Their decrease is not due to our hunting them—they are not often killed by us—but rather to the establishment of the Pax Britannica, which not only allows the native hunters to wander where they like, but also has provided a market, safe to reach with the meat, and at the same time, as a result of the great prosperity prevailing throughout the country, has increased and extended the purchasing power of the inhabitants of towns.

I myself have several times followed elephants, but only once have I ever seen them. I was travelling through my district, and my path lay through a tract of bush close to the Oti river. It is usually my wont to march well ahead of the carriers, accompanied by a native who knows the bush, in case I step off the path to hunt an animal. But this time the man did not know the country, and when I came across the very fresh tracks of a herd of elephants I detailed him to wait and detain the carriers till I came back.

My orderly and myself then went after the herd. After about an hour I came to the conclusion that the elephants had probably gone farther than I could spare the time to follow, and might possibly have left that part altogether, as there were no signs of their having been feeding, only a few trees being uprooted in that mischievous play so peculiar to elephants.

My route had been more or less in the direction I wanted to go, and as I knew that another path lay closer to the river, I decided to take that one. Therefore I sent my orderly back to tell the carriers and I remained alone.

It was close on eight o'clock but not very hot, so I placed my rifle against a tree and sat down on an old white ant-heap some three yards off in a good clearing. The heap was extremely comfortable, having been worn by rain and weather into the semblance of a low arm-chair. There was nothing much to do to while away the time, and nothing likely to come along to disturb me. I had been lying there for about three-quarters of an hour when, on throwing away a burnt-out match, with which I had been lighting my pipe, I glanced up and saw, not fifteen yards away, gazing at me, with ears a-set and head down, the face of an elephant. I slithered (if there is such a word) off the heap to my rifle, and there saw four more making a semicircle round me.

I had not heard a sound of their approach, and, not knowing what was best to do, I ran. The elephants walked by my side, having turned to the right. They neither gained on me nor lost ground : they just kept me company.

After racing what seemed miles, but was probably only two hundred yards or so, I saw a very large and lofty ant-heap. To this I made and got behind it. The elephants stood still, and after a moment or two I decided to shoot. I did, and one fell dead. The others walked up to it and then made off into the bush.

An hour later my carriers arrived. It was a study to watch their faces break from an indifferent appearance into a smile, growing broader until the men laughed aloud for very joy at the certainty of much meat and probable money gain, for they were pretty certain I should give them the body. As for myself, I have never felt so sorry as I did then at having killed an animal. To see the huge mass, of a comparatively harmless character, lying there lifeless after so many years of contented undisturbedness, was in itself a severe reproach. The only interest I got in the subsequent proceedings, which were very savage indeed, was when the stomach was pierced, the sudden releasing of the gases causing a considerable explosion.

The carriers discarded what clothing they had, and the slate-grey body of the elephant soon became a scarlet mass of blood-stained men hacking and pulling at the mountain of red meat. I camped that night near the Oti whilst the carriers heaped up the meat on platforms, which acted as grids. All night they sang and danced the wild dance of the elephant-hunters and hunters in general.

But elephants are becoming very rare on the Gold Coast and its dependencies. In books written two hundred years ago we read of them having been seen and killed within sight of the very sea itself. But the substitution of guns and powder for bows and arrows soon drove them back into the country. There are still a few in the forest, and I once saw there the track of a single elephant. Native hunters occasionally manage to kill one. They walk up to the animal and usually aim at one of the knees. This brings him down, when he can then be easily slain.

In the grass zone, where the animal is easier to detect, the aim is not so restricted, and, as time and distance do not much matter, any place will do. The one I killed had been wounded near the centre of the spine and in the hindquarters.

Elephant stories are not common out here. The best I have heard is that of a D.C. who came across a fine tusker out in the open in the Tumu country. He shot it in the head and it fell, apparently dead. The rest-house was not far away, and he went back for breakfast after having thoroughly examined his kill, even, in his excitement, having sat on it. He sent back his orderly with the villagers and strolled out to watch operations, after having satisfied his hunger. To his surprise he saw the men scattered over the countryside looking for the elephant—it had walked off!

In the north, where there are practically no guns, elephants are killed with bows and arrows and spears. The most ingenious method is for the hunters to sit up in trees and wait while the children drive the herd under the trees, when the hunter hurls himself, together with a stout spear, on to the back of the elephant and then jumps off. This was a favourite practice in the country round Chuchilliga. The spear had a detachable point, so that when the head had once entered the flesh, the shaft would hang loose and help to fluster the animal, whilst the strophanthus with which the point had been dressed infected its blood.

To-day there are no elephants near Chuchilliga, and this very exciting method of hunting is dying out. But sometimes a herd or a portion of a herd will pass within reach, when the old men turn out and prove to a younger generation their skill and their bravery. One such came through this thickly inhabited region when I was D.C. at Zuaragu. One must imagine an undulating country, with here and there small kopjes composed of immense granite boulders. There are few trees, now and then a wood of about a couple of acres, and single baobabs or thorn-trees in the fields. All is cultivated land, with only occasional patches of a short but wiry grass; and spaced apart, at varying ranges of from fifty to two hundred yards from

A PERFORMER AT ZUARAGU.

A Youth of the Nankanni Tribe giving a display at a gathering of the people

each other, flat-roofed houses, somewhat resembling toy forts or sand castles, of a red or grey colour. The population runs to about fifty per square mile, which supports also some ten cows and possibly thirty sheep or goats. There are no towns or villages—not even a sufficient number of these houses close together to justify the term "hamlet." We call this type of house or group of huts a "compound," and they are so numerous that one can march forty-five miles through the districts of Navaro, Zuaragu and Bawku without ever being out of sight of a compound, unless one walks in the bed itself of some stream.

Into this area was driven a herd of elephants from the French country to the north. It numbered thirteen when first sighted on the French side, near a headquarters station called Leo. They were driven mercilessly by the natives, till eventually only four survived. Two were slain in my district.

I was at lunch when a man ran up in a state of great excitement, shouting at me: "Elephant! Elephant!" I said: "Where?" He replied: "At Sambruno." This statement, which seemed almost as foolish as one to the effect that some black-game were settled in Hyde Park, together with the man's wild excitement, inclined me to believe he was mad. I was quite convinced he was when he answered my query as to their number, for he said: "Thousands."

However, a good interpreter had arrived, and he at last learned the whole story, and informed me that two elephants had of a truth been driven into the fields at Sambruno and were still there, and that the people wanted me to kill them, as they feared much damage might be done.

I started at once, galloping off to a place called Via, where I hoped to cut them off, as their route was last reported as lying in that direction. I asked an old woman there if she had seen or heard of any elephant about. She shook her head in a pitying way. I then asked an old man. His reply was: "I am an old man; my fathers and my fathers' fathers lived here. Never have we seen elephant. But if the white man says there are elephant, well, there are elephant here. I have not seen them."

I went back to Zuaragu, where more Sambruno people met me, and asked frantically for help. I was too tired, and not quite sure that the tale was true. However I allowed four mounted constables to go. They were madly keen, and after receiving many warnings from me to be careful how they shot, if many people were about, rode off. That was at five P.M., and Sambruno was nine miles off.

At nine P.M. news reached me that two elephants had been killed, that no man had been hurt, and that they would send in the tusks and tails to me in the morning. Next morning I heard that the constables had arrived too late, that the two elephants were only small ones, and had been completely surrounded by the people, who killed them with arrows and spears and stones. The tusks were indeed small, and had been broken by the stones.

But, as I have said above, to my mind the best hunting by far is that of buffalo, or as we call them out here "bush-cow," the bull being distinguished by the appellation "man bush-cow." It requires very careful hunting to come up with a herd, and usually one stumbles across them without hunting at all. The herd has a knack of leaving a false trail, returning almost on their tracks, and lying in wait or on guard close to their original path.

I was once after buffalo in the Zuaragu district. I had come across their tracks on my march from a place called Naga to Balungo, and decided to follow. After a short trail, easy to trace, we came to stony country very difficult to track in, and with little cover. This was a serious check, so I decided to call off and get along to Balungo, as it was a good distance away. There was a patch of unburned grass close to our path back, and as I came abreast of this, chatting with my hunter, the herd we had been following stampeded inside this grass but not in our view.

I sat down, and after finishing a pipe entered the grass and followed an easy track of broken and bent stems. The patch, as we had known, was a small one, and we slowed up as we drew near the farther side. The hunter climbed a tree to get a view over the open in front of us, and, as he did so, the herd, which had been lying in the grass on our right, having wheeled back to that position, charged. I and the orderly were in the middle, and we took cover behind an ant-heap. It was certainly exciting to hear the great beasts coming and to see the grass bending and waving, and an occasional glimpse of a huge body. Their alarm was of very short duration and they halted with us in their midst. I watched a calf which was standing in an open space and wondered how many "cows" were around, and how many were watching us. Suddenly not twenty yards in front there emerged on to a bare piece of ground, an island as it were in the standing grass, a great bull. He had a magnificent pair of horns and was an easy mark. I fired and he fell. Then there was pandemonium. Cows seemed to be everywhere. The bull was roaring and the cows charged about in all directions. Crouching by the ant-heap, I could just see the bull's form. Presently he stood up and I fired again. Whether I had hit him again I did not know, for he staggered off into the grass bellowing. The others then made off and the bush became suddenly quite still.

We waited twenty minutes or thereabouts, and then followed the wounded bull. He was evidently badly hit, and we came across three places where he had collapsed. But we never got him. The herd had crossed an open space, and had entered the matted river-grass, which was still green, and which presents cover absolutely impenetrable to the human eye. Next day I had to go on, but I persuaded some Frafra to watch the place, and to see if the bull went out with the herd when the latter went to graze. They reported that he had not, but was still in the grass. However, on the following morning he did move, and had wandered down a dry river-bed into the thick cover nearer the Volta, where they dared not follow. I did not blame them. Apparently he recovered, for no sign of him was noticed when eventually the grass was completely burned: a load was taken off my conscience, for there is nothing more damnable than leaving a wounded animal to perish lingeringly in the bush.

Many times have I seen buffalo in full charge; but that was the only time a charge of my own provoking took place. The first time that I saw buffalo at all was when they were in full gallop. That tale, I think, bears telling, as the circumstances in which the incident took place were extraordinary.

I was at the time making a rough survey of a part of the bush which Government was thinking of taking up. I had been following a well-used path, and was accompanied by five natives; two dogs were also with me, but, as there was always a possibility of "meat," they were on leashes. The end of my compass traverse for that day was reached at a convenient spot, where the path went down to a river. This was running between steep banks, and in its bed grew some very dark-leafed trees. I told one of the men to take the dogs down to water whilst I remained above the river in the open. Just as the man started off I heard a leopard cough two or three times, so I called to the man to stop, for the cough came from the river, to which I advanced. I descended into the shade of the trees, which was very dark indeed after the glare above, but could see nothing. A troop of baboons disturbed by the leopard started making a terrible noise, so I presumed the leopard would be somewhere near them; moreover, I rather fancied I could hear him splashing in the water, above which the baboons were. Therefore I climbed up on the other side of the river, accompanied by the men and dogs, and seeing the baboons walked to the bank opposite to where they were raging and shouting. The bank here was sheer. There were no trees in the river-bed and I could see a fine stretch of water. My excitement was intense as I waited for a glimpse of the leopard, whose splashes I now was certain I could hear.

Just then as I peered over the edge I heard a lion roar

not a hundred yards away, and the bush behind me, which was not properly burnt, but still standing, began to wave, and the noise of a stampede of large animals arose. Suddenly I saw above the grass the heads of buffalo, their black horns gleaming and their tails waving. I waited. They tore out into the open and away down the river across a treeless patch into thick river-grass—cows and calves, but no sign of the bull. At last the herd had gone, and only one animal was left. It had not entered the open space, but I had a fair shot and hit it. Unfortunately it proved to be a cow. The bull had apparently been running apart from the herd.

I once saw a herd in full gallop for several hundred yards right in the open. They were all massed together, with a great red-skinned cow in the centre and the bull running by the side of the mass. I had neither gun nor camera with me.

The red bush-cows I do not venture to explain. Usually the coat of the buffalo here is a black tending to a dark grey, but red ones are often seen. The natives hold them in awe and talk often of there being a "queen bush-cow." But if they fear the red one, they are in mortal terror of the albino. These are to be found occasionally, and one is supposed to be the leader of a well-known herd which lives along the Pru near Prang.

To illustrate the fear borne by the natives for irregularly shaped or coloured bush "meat" no better incident can be recorded than the following. Some time ago a soldier went out hunting. He did not return. Search was made. He was found lying in the open, shot through the head. He had with great deliberation and care shot himself. The reason was evident to his finders: there lay dead, killed by him, a pure white kob and a pure white buffalo.

Other animals do not provide so much excitement as the lion, elephant or bush-cow. They are interesting to track, afford good shooting, but far better watching and, if one is lucky, photographing. Both roan and hartebeest have suffered in recent years by a prolonged epizootic of rinderpest. It is more than likely that the disease is spread abroad quite as much by bush "meat" as by domestic herds, for though it is a fact that every herd has its own clearly defined and carefully preserved grazing-ground, yet these pastures overlap. For instance, in a given area of, say, two hundred square miles there will be ordinarily one herd of buffalo, four each of roan and hartebeest, and from eight to ten of kob if a river traverses the country. Now if disease breaks out among these herds, though the animals will not at first leave their ground, water-buck and bush-buck will probably stray across from that area to the next, and it is more than likely that the farthermost herd of kob will graze for only half their area over infected land, and for the other half over non-infected land, thus carrying the disease to the next area.

It is quite interesting to note down the pasturing places of the herds in one's district, and to look them up when there arises the opportunity. Water-buck lend themselves particularly to this, and when once marked down a herd can almost always with certainty be viewed. The same applies also to that beautifully marked little animal the red-flanked duiker, which will regularly use one bush as its resting-place.

Hunting these animals calls for little remark. There is, of course, the thrill of the chase, the satisfaction at the definite completion of a piece of work, the collection of a good head; but far greater than all this I think is to see how near one can get to the herd, how long remain undetected, to watch them at play. There is nothing finer, I think, than to get within, say, anything less than a hundred yards of a herd and watch them settle down; to know that one has them at one's mercy, and to spare them because of their beauty. One has had all the satisfaction of the hunt without that always recurring sense of shame which follows the kill.

The smaller antelopes afford the best meat, and it would be hard to find sweeter flesh than that of the red-fronted gazelle, which is to be found only in the extreme north, where, avoiding the bush proper, they love to frequent the grassy spaces among the fields and compounds. I think it was Sir H. Johnson who suggested that this gazelle was in process of being domesticated at one period. That is certainly a good explanation of this peculiar preference. Fortunately they are very rapid in their movements and are not therefore much troubled by the natives armed only with bows and arrows. It is curious, on first thoughts, that so many should survive, but rabbits at home in England are not very different; moreover, man provides a certain measure of protection.

The gazelle buck are sometimes the reverse of timorous. I knew of one which had been shot at with an arrow by a herd-boy in Kanjaga. The buck turned on him and drove him back to his compound amid the general

A GROUP OF NANKANNI PLAYERS.

The instruments are of hollowed-out gourds, the guitars being covered with iguana skin. The balls are rattles of gourds filled with small stones or seeds.

laughter of many old and young men who watched the incident and never for a moment thought of interfering.

In the extreme south of the Protectorate, where remains of the real forest can be found, and in the forest zone proper, there is that curious little animal the chevrotain. Elsewhere I have mentioned the part it is alleged to play. Hunting it, I should imagine, is impossible for a European. When first I heard of it I was told that it was a brother to a duiker—*i.e.* of the same family—but that it lived mostly in the water, and was almost invisible, as only a small part of its head was to be seen as it swam, and when it did this it usually kept among the reeds and bushes, so that only very rarely was it seen at all. Moreover, it had no horns, but fangs, and preferred a diet of fish to leaves or grass! I asked if a specimen could be brought me. Two were. They had fangs, not horns; they were marked similarly to the harnessed antelope; were obviously, to judge from their coats, water-living animals, and there were no signs of grass or leaves in their stomachs. They are trapped, and never to the knowledge of my informers had been shot. I did not see the traps, so cannot describe them.

But in all this hunting there are two essentials: one must have a good hunter with one—not only to pick up the trail but also to find the way back, for when one is concentrated on hunting one soon loses sense of direction—and one should have a good dog.

My dogs will be remembered in another chapter; of my hunters I could never adequately write. They became my friends, and who would publish his feelings towards his friends? But there is one thing always to remember.

They do not repeat, when one misses badly, those famed words of the gillie:

"It was nae my fault; it was nae the fault of the rifle, for she is a good 'un; it was nae the veasibility, for the light was pairfect; and it was nae the fault of the stag; but ye've missed him clean."

Rather will my African blame the antelope. It had too much "medicine" and succeeded in twisting the gun.

CHAPTER X

ANTS & INSECT LIFE

TO me, in my solitude, the most interesting of hobbies is the collection and observation of insects. There is no end to the interest one can take in this hobby; but one feels lamentably ignorant of the subject, and it is only as an amateur that I venture to give these notes.

Perhaps ants are the most noticeable of all insects in West Africa. There are so many millions of them, and they usually are so persistent with their stings and bites and tickling, that one must pay attention to them.

Foremost of all ants are those known as "driver ants"—their habit of driving all before them accounts for the name. Everyone in West Africa who has been in the bush at all is familiar to a certain extent with these ants, and tales of the wonders they perform are innumerable.

I noticed them on my first day in the bush. Across my path lay a black rope of a width of some two inches. A closer scrutiny showed a stream of black ants, three, four or five abreast, proceeding at a good rate between a double hedge of larger ants who, like lines of soldiers, guarded the passing procession. These hedges were very thick, but I have never quite made out how they are formed. The ants are nearly erect, and interlocked, forming almost a canopy for the marchers; their antennæ wave ceaselessly in the air and their mandibles are open, ready to attack any intruder who may threaten to break the line.

No man whom I have met has ever seen the beginning or the end of this procession, nor have I ever seen the forming of the "hedge," though many times I have watched the repairing of a breach. These lines seem endless. I have seen a line continuing across a road for over forty-eight hours—but I had seen neither its commencement nor its end. The rate of march is, according to several tests I have made, just over a yard a minute. Averaging four abreast, there must have passed in forty-eight hours, any given point, at least 1,658,880 ants, each a quarter of an inch in length, and, in addition, the double hedge must be reckoned in. This would give close on 4,000,000 ants in the formic army; and every one bites, some of them very severely.

The ants themselves can be divided into several classes. There are small workers, armed with a light pair of mandibles; there is a larger class of worker, and there are at least three varieties of the "soldier" ant, distinguishable from the worker by a much larger, almost armour-plated thorax, and with mandibles of great strength and size, almost out of proportion to the rest of the body. The leader of the army, or the queen ant, I have never seen.

Often have I seen these ants at work in their hunting. They feed on anything living, but apparently are not grain or fruit or cooked-meat eaters. At Goaso I had my house attacked five days in one week, and was forced to abandon it for the time being. I had thus quite early in my career a good opportunity to observe some of the methods adopted by these insects.

One evening I saw a line of ants approaching one of my lawns from the bush. When the head of the army, which was not walking between ant "hedges," reached the border round the grass it divided into two, one line marching at right angles to the other. When these lines stretched some ten yards down the sides of the lawn, ants rapidly detached themselves and entered the grass, but the line itself continued. I then noticed other lines converging on my garden, until I counted nine from where I had taken my stance. This was about a quarter of an hour from the time I had first seen the ants at all.

By now the grass—which was doubh, and about a foot deep—was all movement: grasshoppers, stick-insects, caterpillars, butterflies, moths, flies were all in motion, and over all a mass of almost invisible, hurrying ants. No ant seemed to bother about killing any particular insect. A bite, and the ant passed on. Thus even butterflies were killed. One bite, and the insect flew a short way, only to meet another ant, who gave a second bite. Gradually the formic acid overcame the wretched insect until it fell, and was immediately dissected by the ants in the ground and its pieces removed to the lines outside the lawn border, where the ants, laden with the body or a leg, fell in without halting and followed the loadless ants who had not yet entered the hunt. Caterpillars, great beetles, everything was thus treated. But, although I watched the hunt closely, I could not detect the moment when the ants had finished their work and gone on their marauding way.

The following morning I watched the ants moving off in their seemingly endless line with the double row of guardian soldiers. Then I witnessed a very interesting spectacle. Where the ants were crossing the path was settled a grey fly, a little larger than our own blue-bottles. The fly kept about eight inches off the ant "hedges," and was obviously intently watching the procession, though I cannot make out how it could see through the ranks. The procession of marchers consisted as usual of smaller ants in threes and fours and fives, but now each ant was laden with spoil. Whenever a nice fat piece of insect was being carried past, the fly left his post and swooped lightly over the uplifted antennæ of the soldier ants. By continually annoying them thus, the fly succeeded in breaking the ranks, whose units scattered over the neighbouring bare ground searching for the cause of the annoyance. Having thus broken the "hedge" the fly by very careful swoops drew the ant carrying the coveted morsel away from the others, and steered it to a space free of ants. The fly then proceeded to pull at the ant's spoil. The ant, to defend its load, had to release hold, and as the morsel was loosed the fly at once pounced on it, but the ant managed to secure a grip in time. There then ensued a tug-of-war, and eventually the fly won, and flew off with its booty. Meanwhile the ant soldiers had closed their ranks again, but the ant carrier, after a short deliberation, approached the "hedge" and the ranks opened to allow it to pass and resume its place, although loadless, in the procession.

I have watched this many times. Always has the fly won.

On another occasion I watched an even more interesting attack on a line of " drivers " returning laden with spoil from a foray. There is a red ant, a tree-dweller, whose bite is exceptionally painful. I think everyone in West Africa knows this ant. It makes a nest by weaving together a number of leaves, and shows a marked preference for mango-trees. At Krachi there are several avenues of mango-trees, and these red ants swarm everywhere.

On the occasion referred to I had come across a line of " drivers " hastening home. I stopped to see if the grey fly was at work, but instead saw the red ants stationed at intervals in companies all along the line. These companies were actually attacking the column. Two or three would hurl themselves on the " hedges," which broke to repel the attack. Most of the red ants would remain in company, but individuals rushed out from time to time and bit and slew a soldier driver. Another would penetrate the marching column, seize a carrier with its load and actually carry it out of the line. Meanwhile the soldier drivers were engaged in a death-to-death struggle with red ants, who, if being worsted, were reinforced by others from their company. Many on both sides were slain, and the dead were left *in situ*. It was obvious that the red ant was the stronger and could resist two or even three soldier drivers. But when hard pressed it must have had some means of sending out an S.O.S., for assistance usually came to it, and if it was relieved, one would see it wander off the field and nurse its wounds. I saw a very gallant stand by some ten red ants who were completely surrounded by soldier drivers. I could not count these latter, but should imagine there were at least fifty of them.

That band of red ants perished to the last one, but there was a far greater heap of dead drivers round them.

I did not observe what was done with the spoil taken from the spoilers. I rather think other driver ants took it back, and that the red ants were attacking either for sheer love of fighting or to impress on the drivers that they were trespassing on an area reserved to the red ants and that future offence would be more severely punished. Neither could I see any co-operation between the various companies of red ants, only individuals of the same company helping one another.

But these drivers are not content with insects only. They will attack, and generally succeed in killing, anything living. A fowl-run has to be very carefully watched; chained-up animals, even the smaller mammals, will be killed, picked clean, and divided into portable morsels. Snakes are often killed by the ants, and to see these reptiles scurrying before an onslaught is by no means a rare sight.

An Ashanti hunter gave me a graphic description of the slaying of a python by these Lilliputian Huns. It would seem incredible, if one forgot that pythons are slow to be aroused after one of their meals, and that the ants, attacking in myriads, would have injected enough formic acid by the time the python was awakened to dull his wits, and quite possibly would have blinded it.

Once I witnessed ants enter a village. The attacked portion was abandoned by the inhabitants, who removed all their live stock and then made a barrier of hot ashes and embers across the village, for that is the only barrier these drivers cannot cross. Water is useless, for the larger soldier ants lock their legs and make an ant-bridge over which the rest can pass. This chain is very deftly swung into the current, and by the struggles of the ants is carried across to the other side.

Now it is a curious fact that the driver ants when attacking a man do not bite at once. If one disturbs a line of march they will bite immediately they can find flesh; but only when one is quite covered with them during a hunt do they begin to bite. This maddens one, and possibly explains how animals become an easy prey, for their thinking power is dulled in an effort to deal with the biters, and so the road to escape is not taken in time.

A short time ago the D.C. at Ejura witnessed an amusing incident. Three white men were his guests and he had left them on the verandah for a moment or two. On his return he found them stark naked, swearing and busily picking off ants. From personal experience I know that nothing short of rapid undressing can deal with an attack. The ants will soon leave one's empty clothes.

There are other black ants whose habits closely resemble those of the driver, but it is only the latter that is to be feared. I do not think it is found much north of the eighth parallel.

But there is one species of ant to be seen everywhere in the country. It is of a dark grey colour, and marches in a column, three, four or five abreast. The column is not protected by lined-up soldiers, and is only two to six feet long. The ant itself is much larger than the driver, and measures about half-an-inch. There are no classes, so far as I could observe, and all the ants resemble each other. It is more than likely that one colony of these ants will send out several columns on forays whilst the workers and queens remain at home, but one cannot spare the time to observe this, and one can only trust to luck to solve the problem. This ant is of a very beneficial character, as it lives on the so-called white ants. Often have I watched the column reach a white ants' nest. A halt is made. The column suddenly breaks up; the individual ants race at the nest, enter by the various openings, and in two minutes or less emerge holding a white ant. Each individual ant holds one. The column is re-formed and well away before the soldier white ants come out to see what all the fuss is about. Only once have I seen these soldiers in time to fight the raiders; and when one of them does catch a raider the latter is killed, and the body carried into the nest.

Before leaving the subject of ants it may perhaps be of interest to record the work of a small spider, commonly known as the ant-lion. It lives in the ground, where it bores a small hole, ejecting the earth, finely crushed or chewed, and quite dry, until the hole is more or less concealed at the bottom of a crater. An ant passing by, if unwary, will slip on the edge of the crater; an avalanche ensues, carrying with it the unfortunate ant. Every effort by the ant to get out of the crater results in further avalanches, which the spider concealed at the bottom assists by kicking up more sand, covering the ant at times, and repairing the walls of the crater. The spider uses its back pair of legs for this. Eventually the ant is exhausted and is seized by the spider.

Wasps are quite as interesting as ants, especially the

mason wasps, which make mud tubes for their eggs and then bring caterpillars and grubs on which the wasp larva is to feed. But I am no Fabre to describe these wonders—one can only watch the insects occasionally, and remain astonished at their diligence and real maternal care.

These wasps are not the yellow-and-black-striped ones of England. They are great black insects, very attenuated, with a long thin waist and an awe-inspiring sting. So far I have escaped, for, although these wasps are seen in practically every room, they do no harm unless disturbed. Natives aver that if one breaks these mud houses of the wasps, ill-luck will follow. That seems probable enough, and possibly children are thereby deterred from meddling with them.

Other wasps are numerous. In the far northern parts one reaches the thorn-bush country, beyond the orchard-bush. Many of these bushes are a mass of hanging wasp-nests, quite small. The egg-cells are visible, but a close examination has never been made by me. The wasps are too vicious—little brown insects, with yellow bands round the abdomen, and a very nasty sting. Natives have a very wholesome respect for them, but usually do not run away when they upset the inhabitants of a nest, as the wasps will follow. I saw Kojo once standing stark naked, with his cloth on the ground. I asked what he was doing and he shouted to me to keep away. The boy remained perfectly still, and after some time slowly picked up his cloth and, putting it on, walked away. He had six or seven stings, but told me that if nothing more disturbed the wasps, after their first defensive attack, they would soon calm down. That is why he had stripped and "frozen."

There is another wasp—a solitary person. It is a very large insect, of a magnificent blue-black colour and with a flaming red tail. To see it is enough to make one afraid. It lives in small holes in the ground and feeds on caterpillars. The drumming of its wings is very loud and somewhat alarming.

But the bees are more interesting perhaps than wasps. They are of a smaller type than our own, and live in holes in trees or in the ground. They are almost domesticated in places, especially in the Dagomba country, where pots, calabashes and hollow wooden pipes are set up in trees to entice a wild swarm to settle and make honey. This is taken, both in daylight and at night, by the natives, who proceed naked to the nest and keep off the bees with smoke, with the result that the honey often tastes of the smoke and fire, and has usually to be strained before we can eat it. At present the beeswax finds a better market locally than a sale to European merchants.

Bees are the insects which the natives fear above all others. When angered they are very vicious, and have been known quite often to kill men and cattle. There lies at Wa a European thus slain. Once my convoy was attacked by a swarm which had their nest in a tree, and had been disturbed by the noise of the carriers' talk. The whole column was routed, and many very badly stung; but none of them threw down the loads they were carrying. They are mostly brave men. However, the flag was dropped right where the bees were most numerous. A constable, who formed part of the escort, stopped, and rescued it. Fortunately it was furled and the bunting did not flap, for otherwise the man would quite possibly have lost his life.

Twice have I had to lie flat down on the ground to allow a swarm to pass, and on one occasion my horse was just behind me. The bees were all over him but he never moved, nor even flicked his tail. Animals apparently understand the bees as well as the natives.

Among the latter are certain individuals who have a marvellous flair for these insects. They are usually hunters, who are accustomed to spend much time in the uninhabited bush. Naturally they cannot be hampered with the carrying of a quantity of food, and they rely to a large extent on wild honey.

There is a certain bird—I have never seen it close—which acts as a detector of bees' nests. Whenever the man sees one of these birds he follows it, and in a short while locates the nest to which the bird has led him. The rest is simple, and the hunter mixes the honey with water, which he drinks, and presumably gains from it considerable sustenance.

But perhaps the greatest nuisance caused by bees is a vile habit of theirs to nest in our houses. Year after year they will return—I do not know, of course, if in reality the same swarm comes back—and one's house becomes full of them. They do not as a rule attack one, but there is always the risk that one may annoy them.

I knew a D.C. who was put in a great quandary by bees. They entered his local prison and took up their abode near the door. The prison consisted of a large single room, with two barred windows and a large iron-barred door. There were six prisoners in at the time, whose sentences varied from two weeks to three months.

On his daily visit to see if all was well he asked if the prisoners had any complaints, and they answered no, save that they did not like the bees. His inspection of the nest unfortunately disturbed them, and he, warder and prisoners fled precipitately from the jail. There was no other place to put his prisoners that night. Therefore he had to put them on parole to return next morning at six, and allowed them to stay the night in the village. They all reported at the time fixed.

Akin to bees and wasps are the termites, or white ants. Of these there are many varieties. Some make their nests mushroom- or umbrella-shaped, about two feet high; others build great homes, pinnacled and towered, even twenty feet high; others nest in the mud walls of our houses or in the rafters. They are a terrible pest, and the damage they do is incredible. Practically anything, except metal, left for a while in contact with the floor or walls will be devoured. Curiously enough, though, the shell of the article remains, and is to all intents and purposes quite all right, but as soon as one touches it, it will fall to pieces.

A certain variety of white ant is eagerly sought for by the natives as food for their chickens, which they will carry out to their fields in baskets and place down near a nest, already broken so that the inmates are exposed. Not all white ants are good for fowls, and if one makes a mistake there is a risk of losing the bird.

Another variety is eaten by the people. This termite makes its flight on the sultry evenings after a downpour of rain. In Ashanti the children are the chief consumers of this dish, but in the north everyone is fond of these insects. The method of capture is curious, and I have watched it scores of times.

Whenever the evening seems a likely one parties set out from their houses carrying flaming torches of grass. A flight of males from the nest is soon located, a space near by is cleared, a little basin hollowed out and a fire lit round the clearing. The insects, attracted by the light, fly into the circle in hundreds, and their wings are either scorched off as they cross the fire or fall off from the frantic blows the blinded insect gives them in an effort to rise from the ground. The watchers sweep them into the basin and, clearing away some of the fire, fill calabashes or baskets with the crawling insects. They are eaten either roasted or boiled or raw. I have seen boys eat them alive; and have been told that they are quite sweet.

But of all the white ants the great prize is the queen ant of that variety which builds a cathedral-like nest. I know of a white man who ate one once. He averred that it was really excellent fried and reminded him of marrow with a flavour of nuts. He had a stomach of iron, that man, for of all loathly insects assuredly the queen white ant is the loathliest. She is of an enormous size, running from two to as much as four inches from her head to her tail. The head is a small one, not much larger than that of our own wood ants, but the body is swollen like a blood-full tick, is a dirty creamy—almost transparent—colour, and has a few scattered brown hairs on it. It is hard work to find one, and necessitates as a rule much digging. The diggers have to be careful too of the soldier white ants, who are armed with extraordinarily powerful mandibles. Usually the queen is close to the bottom of the nest, where are a number of more or less rounded stones, made by the ants. These stones give a certain quantity of lime, and would be of use in building if one could extract a purer combination of sand and lime. In the absence of lime, during the war, I heard that the Roman Catholic Fathers in Nyassaland used these ant-manufactured pebbles quite successfully. I experimented at Navaro, but could not attain the correct mixture.

The above insects can be observed by everyone who comes to West Africa. Others are not so easy. There are the dragonflies, usually of very beautiful shades, but unsatisfactory to collect, as their colours so soon fade; stick and leaf insects of every variety: some like straws, some like leaves, others like seeds and grains; flies and gnats, harmful and harmless, which would require a volume for themselves to describe, anathematize but not to laud.

But, as elsewhere, it is the moths and butterflies which appeal most to one. Easy to catch and easy to preserve, they form a collection the most beautiful to make and to display.

For some years now I have spent my evenings collecting them, and I know of no more attractive way of spending the early night hours, when one seeks relaxation from work. One cannot, however, collect exactly as one does in England, where breeding from caterpillars, treacling trees, using lights, even trapping them, beating for them, are the ordinary methods of procedure. It is not possible to remain in one's station for a long enough time to ensure proper feeding and care of the caterpillars, and I doubt if one could train a native boy to watch them and guard them from their myriad enemies. Treacling might be successful, were it not for the ants and lizards and other moth-eaters. Lights attract bats and spiders and mantis beetles as well as moths, so, unless one keeps the lamp in one's own room, light-traps are useless. Beating is impossible. Snakes and wasps see to that.

As for butterflies, there is not so much difficulty. If the heat is too great to stay out in the sunshine, it is quite easy to train a boy to catch them and not to injure his captures. And what wonderful catches one does make! Colours indescribable, delicacy and crudeness of shape unimagined. There are scarlet butterflies as large as our own meadow-browns, golden ones shot with green and silver, blue ones of a wonderful brightness, tailed ones like our swallow-tails, and others with tails longer than the butterfly itself, adorned with a peacock's eye at the end.

In the shaded forest paths they rise without ceasing as one strolls along—dun ones, bright ones, variegated ones. Some seem to glide more silently than others and fade out of sight into the surrounding darkness of the forest; others more brilliantly hued prefer the spaces where some fallen giant of the woods has let in the sunshine; others are to be found only where a leopard or a cat has passed, just as the Purple Emperors prefer putrid meat or filth. These last are usually seen only when the heat is greatest, for the large wild cats like to wander along man's paths when man is taking his siesta in the middle of the day.

At every stream where puddles or damp earth are found thousands arise at one's approach. Sometimes they seem to be all of one species, large white-and-orange ones, black-and-green swallow-tails, and another *papilio* of greater delicacy, a light green, blue and black. Rotting fruit is another favourite feeding-place, and here the darker ones fly up in such numbers that one verily might think the earth's surface to be alive.

At Sunyanî there was, during September, a curious flight of butterflies every day at about two P.M. It lasted nearly an hour. The butterfly somewhat resembled our grayling, and they flew in a jerky flight from about a yard to twenty feet or so in the air in thousands, always from the north southward. Whence they came or whither they went I know not.

In the northern parts the butterflies are not so numerous, nor so brilliantly hued. I think that the annual burning of the grass accounts to a large extent for this, since butterflies, which are mostly hibernating during the dry season, can hardly escape the flames, no matter whether they are pupating or in the larva stage or in the imago.

Butterflies have not interested me so much as moths. They are better known, and more generally collected, on account of their beauty. Moths I have collected from earliest childhood, and they afford me out here a real relaxation. Occasionally one can catch specimens in the net during the daylight, but obviously this is very occasional. So far I have employed only two methods of capture: visiting fermenting fruit and enticing by lamps, set indoors.

A mango-tree or, better, an avenue of such trees, when the fruit has ripened and fallen, is a marvellous sight at night-time. The whole ground where the fruit is rotting is a moving mass of almost intoxicated moths. I have at Krachi nearly three miles of these trees, and as one walks down the avenue with a lantern the air seems full of heavy-bodied, awkward-flying moths. For only about a fortnight does this last, and then, when the moon is up, the moths seem to have gone away altogether, for moths out here, as at home, do not like moonlight.

Later one gets the fruit from the wild fig-trees. There used to be one alongside my bungalow. For one week there was a brilliant display of large moths, with yellow and brown upper wings and vermilion under wings. But collecting under trees has its drawbacks. There are scores of scorpions to avoid, and an occasional snake. Ants, of course, swarm, and often one is just defeated in a capture by a company of ants, or a frog or a bat.

Enticing moths by strong lamplight into one's room or verandah is the easier way, and on sultry nights, with a light rain falling, or just after a shower, it is quite exciting, and as the moths come in in numbers one gets quite tired. My best night was one hundred and sixty-eight specimens between eight P.M. and midnight, comprising one hundred and one different species. That was a night ideal for collecting. There was no moon; it was very sultry; slight rain was falling; and the month was October, just after the heavy rains, for moths are far less numerous in the dry season or in the big rains.

I had trained Kojo to collect for me, and rarely an evening passed in the station without his bringing in a specimen new to me. His memory of what I had already collected was quite extraordinary, for moths to the natives are usually just moths, and no differentiation is made, whereas the butterflies each have their native names amongst the children (men state they have forgotten them). This can readily be understood, for the native does not, as a rule, stay up late, and when he does he has no lamp sufficiently strong, and therefore he is not familiar with them.

There are drawbacks to this way of collecting. One is tempted to stay up very late in the hope of getting the really large ones, which seem to emerge only after midnight—which fact, I think, may be explained by their being very slow fliers, and therefore an easy prey to bats; and the appetite of these latter is by then probably already satiated.

Another disadvantage is that one's room is filled with other insects, especially the large-winged ants commonly called "sausage-flies." Beetles galore also visit one, and become a great nuisance, with their noisy flight and continual crashes, due to their being blinded by the light. Lizards and spiders and bats arrive uninvited. The first eventually becomes quite tame and friendly, and will take food from one's hand; the second, unless they are tarantulas or of other biting species, are beneficial and keep down flies, and possibly mosquitoes; the third have to be driven out, as every dweller in the tropics knows, for they will settle in the roof, breed there, and render the place almost uninhabitable.

The quickness of these insect-hunters is remarkable. Some of the spiders seem to upset the theory of gravity, for they will leap from the wall at a moth, catch it in the air, and land again on the wall. The lizards can catch a moth in their mouths at an incredible distance, scarcely seeming to move their heads. The bats catch them on the wing and at one bite swallow the body, while the severed wings fall to the ground.

Sometimes one has to race them for a prize; but my greatest disappointment was with a very pretty small moth, which I had been examining. I turned to get a cyanide-of-potassium bottle, and when I looked round I was just in time to see a mouse catch my moth. Another and more interesting competitor is the mantis.

Most people are familiar with these so-called praying insects. To watch them catch and devour a moth is quite grim. The mantis squats, so to speak, on its third pair of legs, and holds its front paws in an attitude of prayer. All the time it keeps screwing round its head as if it were on a swivel, seeking for a meal. Presently it will move towards a moth resting in the glare. When within range it halts, and suddenly thrusts out the front pair of legs and catches the moth, which it will hold to its mouth with both "hands," and slowly and deliberately eat the unfortunate insect alive.

Of the moths I have taken this is no place to record a list, but one or two captures afforded more interest than usual. I was once in bed with a slight attack of fever, and had kept a lamp by the bedside. I had dozed off, but was awakened by a noise that was peculiarly familiar. It was that strange squeak which the death's-head moth makes, and I caught a very fine specimen. On another occasion I had asked for some cuttings of oleander from Coomassie, which was close on four hundred miles away. Five of the plants throve, and on one of them was an egg of the oleander hawk-moth. That egg hatched, and in course of time I killed at lamplight a very fine specimen of the moth.

To a collector it is very regrettable that one cannot keep caterpillars. There are any quantity to be found, but apart from the difficulty, already mentioned, of feeding them and protecting them, there is a considerable risk of urtication. One sees some curious caterpillars of quite eccentric shape. In particular there is a grey-white hairless one which feeds on yam roots. It is when full grown nearly five inches long, and has the curious habit of wriggling along on its back, with its feet waving in the air. Another variety is a hairy one of a beautiful golden colour. It marches about in company, forming an unbroken line, each except the leader keeping its head in closest touch with the preceding one's stern. If one takes one away from the line, the portion of the column cut off closes up at once, and the subtracted caterpillar, when released, will, after a rapid survey, join up at the rear of the column. I have never put one down more than eighteen inches from the rest, so I do not know how far off it can be before it loses complete touch.

In the north of the Protectorate, where the shea-trees are mostly to be found, is a moth of which the larva feeds on the shea leaves. It is a brown-and-white caterpillar of a fair size, and hairy. The eggs are laid in May or June, and the larva emerges towards the end of June or middle of July. In August the heavy rains fall, when it hibernates, to reappear at the end of September. During October it attains a large size, and being generally in great armies will completely strip the shea-trees of all verdure. It pupates during November and the imago issues during May.

Caterpillars sometimes swarm, and have been known to become quite a plague. In 1906 the French territory bordering on the north of the Proctectorate was largely devastated, and the millet and guinea-corn destroyed, with the result that a serious famine ensued. In 1921 my then district of North Mamprussi was in many parts laid quite bare during the month of May. The early millet, which tides over the gap between the end of June and the main crop harvested in November, had just sprouted, and the whole country, for most of the district is under cultivation, was really looking very fine. I had to leave Zuaragu to meet the Chief Commissioner, and three weeks later came into that station in his company. He asked me how it was that the whole countryside round about was bare, whereas the rest of the district was looking fresh and green. Unthinkingly I replied that the crops were probably ground-nuts and would not be up yet. That satisfied him and me, but not my assistant, who, after we had seen the Chief out of the district, asked me about the ground-nuts, and pointed out a field of millet which was obviously being destroyed by something. We got off our horses to look, and saw the place was swarming with caterpillars. It may seem a travellers' tale to relate that we actually heard them, and quite distinctly too, eating the leaves.

This seemed serious, and a meeting of the chiefs was

called. They said they had heard of a similar occurrence, but had no suggestions. Rain was the only remedy, but the rain-makers (*saa-dana*) seemed unsuccessful. Two evenings later a heavy tornado came, with very violent rain, and the caterpillars were killed, beaten and drowned to death. Every rut or gutter was a mass of dead larvæ. Previously I had watched them carefully. There were two species, and several ichneumon flies, which I saw actually on the larvæ, were laying their eggs between the segments of the caterpillars.

I have mentioned scorpions in this chapter as something to be on one's guard against when collecting. In the forest zone they are not so numerous as in the north. There are two, possibly three, varieties: one, a large black one, which attains eleven inches (the largest I ever saw that another European had captured), is chiefly a denizen of the forest lands; the other, a brown or yellow one, with which most people are familiar, and which is very common indeed and can be found at any time after a short search under stones, is met with throughout the Sudanese or grass zone. One has only to watch a native pick up a stone to see how common the latter type is; the extreme care taken shows that "once bitten, many times very shy" is very true indeed. But certain natives claim to be immune to their stings and will readily handle them; and most of us have witnessed one such native actually place the brutes in his mouth. That is by no means an uncommon show in the markets. Any scorpion will be taken. However, the most remarkable case of immunity I ever came across was in a market-place close to the French frontier, called Paga. A local native there, who sported trousers and a coat on market-days, had had his pockets picked on two or three occasions. He put into one pocket four or five scorpions, and later dropped into it openly some coins. The thief saw this. He was not immune, and was brought to me still in great agony. The prosecutor showed me that this story was true by actually going outside the court and lifting some stones till he found two scorpions, which he picked up and put in his pocket, quite regardless as to how he handled them.

CHAPTER XI

SACRIFICE, WITCHCRAFT & HYENAS

BEFORE leaving these generalities, a paragraph more or less descriptive of sacrificing may not be amiss. On several occasions have I witnessed these, where individuals are concerned, but have never tried to attend one of the communal gatherings. Many informants assure me that save for the number present the procedure is the same. In the following instance the suppliant wished to make an offering to the earth-god at a place called Sirigu, in the Nankanni country. Now the earth-god resided or had his temple in a certain grove not far from the Government Rest-House. I had been inside the wood often enough, and by following the numerous tracks had found the actual sacrificing spot. It was beneath one of the taller trees, and round about the ground had been swept and kept clear of grass and weeds. The earth-god had a priest—the *tindada*, or owner of the land—who accompanied the suppliant. I asked if I might attend, or, rather, if my presence would interfere with the ceremony. The question astonished them, and was apparently a needless one. There was very little ceremony. Its simplicity struck me most. The two men squatted down in front of the stone, and the priest called to the Spirit of the Earth saying:

"Father, Father, come! This man Aiyamaga has

brought you a fowl. Father, receive it and may his wife soon get better." Three times he repeated the prayer, the suppliant holding the fowl on its back on the stone with his right hand in such a manner that it could not flutter. The priest then pulled the fowl's head a bit, so that the throat was exposed. This he cut, and, leaving some feathers on the stone with the blood, threw away the head, whilst the suppliant released the body, which fluttered away. The two watched this carefully, to see which way it would die, for if it died on its back the omen was good, the god had accepted the present. If the fowl died otherwise then the present had been refused. It is curious that this rule obtains right through from the forest to the limits of the sand belt—all authorities concur.

There is no need to give further examples. They are all alike in their simplicity and in their straightforwardness. As to the rest of the proceedings in the public sacrifices, they are more in the nature of general rejoicings at large gatherings than of a ceremonial character. But I hope later to enlarge on this.

In addition to the above-outlined faith there are several beliefs—substrata, so to speak, of the spiritual edifices erected by these people. These do not partake so much of the nature of religion as of superstition—terms almost interchangeable. But it is difficult to draw a line.

One frequently hears praises of the savage life, extolling their contentment, their freedom from the hurry and noise and worry of modern life. That is a delusion. Both our so-called civilized life and that of so-called savages are full of endless worry; both are bound by the strongest of fetters, fashioned in the fire of convention; both are troubled by the curse of man, incessant labour. Maybe we have outgrown some of the superstitions which form such a burden to savage man; maybe—if one were a cynic one might well write "undoubtedly"—we are about to attain his stage of culture. In any case, if we have lost them, we have found others equally as irksome, equally as strong.

It is not so long ago that we all believed witches could change themselves into wild beasts. It seems ridiculous; but still, we did believe it: we knew for a fact that such terrible happenings did occur. The native here is as equally positive on this point as we used to be. There is no need to argue the question, it is a question of faith.

Such beasts—sometimes man, sometimes animal, interchanging their forms at will—are known as wer-wolves. The following incidents will show how widespread this belief is.

When I was at Goaso a certain chief, whom I had got to know well, told me one evening, in answer to a query as to his health, that he was very worried. He had had bad news; two of his friends in distant villages were seriously ill; it was his fault, and he did not know what to do. Asked to explain, he averred that of late, when he went to sleep at night-time, he had assumed the shape of an enormous bat—a winged crocodile he described—and had visited these and other friends, and had been eating them; hence their illness; what was my advice? Now he firmly believed this, and offered many sacrifices. The dream kept on recurring and, as its substance was common knowledge, public opinion at his suicide a few months later, after I had been transferred, was that he had been a wizard; that he knew it, and that he had taken his life in a rather heroic way. Koja was my informant of the last, for I always kept in friendly touch with my erstwhile people.

A second case that came directly to my notice was not actually in my district. I had gone to visit the D.C. at Wioso, and in one of his villages the elders, accompanied by most of the people, came to me for advice. They stated they were at night leopards, and that they lived on human flesh (spiritually, it must be understood) whilst in that guise; that many people whom they had thus eaten were dying in neighbouring villages; that they had been accused of this witchcraft before their head chief, and having pleaded guilty had been told to make certain large sacrifices; these they had made, but their bad habits still continued; could I help them?

The belief persisted, and in the end the village resolved to break up and disperse. This they did, but whether they still in imagination continued their nightly debauches in their supposed guise of leopards I know not.

In the north the commonest type of wer-wolf is the wer-hyena. I know of no man of the Northern Territories who is not absolutely convinced that men do change quite often into hyenas. Of course this animal is not the only one. In another book I have related how a village in the Bura country was certain that they were all sometimes elephants. And it is of interest to record that a man-eating lion is not even called a lion, for everyone knows that only a bewitched lion will eat man. It is, therefore, not a lion but a lion-disguised witch.

It is not difficult to understand how a hyena is the

more usual animal for a witch to change into. I think it is pretty clear that the spirit of the man does not enter into the body of a hyena: it changes into the animal and the human body is for the moment gone. In Ashanti I think —though I speak very guardedly—that the spirit of the man leaves the body and adopts a spiritual animal skin. This is a point extremely difficult to discuss with people. They are very sensitive in the matter, as one would suppose, since the accusation of being a witch is not a popular one.

Hyenas are in many ways closely connected with man. They are practically the only animal of prey which regularly frequents the neighbourhood of man. They visit the market-places night after night, scavenge around the houses, raid the sheep and goats, kill dogs, and howl and laugh in the very streets. They slink away with a growl at man's approach, but they do not go far. They are often seen standing like a man on their hind legs.

Although I may be reproached with digressing, I think the following stories may not be amiss in connexion with hyenas. They will serve to illustrate how closely they are in touch with man, and perhaps help to account for their being chosen, more than other animals, as the animal into which witches are wont to change.

A certain officer leaving Tamale for Tolon, the first halting-place on the road to Wa, was overtaken by darkness. He was a trifle nervous of his horse and walked in front, leading the animal. He remembered how on the last occasion when he had done the same, and the circumstances had been similar, a pair of hyenas had suddenly leaped out of a rubbish-pit, growling, and had frightened him and his horse. Suddenly, as these thoughts passed through his brain, he lifted his head, for he had been picking his way on a dark path through high grass, and saw a hyena standing on its hind legs, face to face with him. The hyena growled, and the man hit out with his left, hitting the hyena full in the jaw. It fell down, and the man overbalancing came on top. There was a scuffle, and the hyena said: "Massa, massa!" It was the postman from Wa!

I have seen hyenas in broad daylight on three or four occasions. This is not a usual sight, and my native guides have always been perturbed, especially as I have failed to kill. On one occasion I left the camp at six-thirty in the morning accompanied by two men. I was moving on to the next village, my carriers going along the road and myself with the two hunters making a detour to see the country and to get "meat" if possible.

Shortly after seven—the sun being then well up—a hyena howled. This was a very unusual occurrence. The sound came from a stream not far away, which, although not running, owing to the dry season being well advanced, yet contained a few pools. I decided, more for diversion than any other reason, to go down to see if we could find any tracks. These were soon located, good fresh spoor. I followed, and told the two men to come after me, but take care not to lose the trail. This was not difficult to trace, and I went ahead at a fair pace. I knew the country would soon become quite open and there was a remote chance of viewing the hyena. (There is no sport in hunting these brutes, but I hate them, as they are so cruel in their killing, and I hoped I might get it.) Presently the spoor came out of the grass into a bare sandy space, without a blade of grass or bush or any growth whatsoever. The track lay across this, and to my surprise it suddenly changed into the track of man. For a few moments I cast about to see where the animal had turned and whence the man had come, but as my two followers were by now quite close I turned back and told them I would go after "meat." I did not want their superstitious fears aroused, and so spoil the hunting. I need not have worried, for when I told them one answered: "Oh yes; we knew it was a man. No real hyena is out when the sun is up. But we wanted you to kill the witch."

That nearly happened at Tumu. The D.C.'s house there is not very far from the prison guard-house, which we term "fort." The D.C. had been disturbed on several nights by the howling of a hyena. He asked the guard if they had seen it and they replied they had, and that the animal regularly came nosing around a midden—euphemistically termed incinerator—a few yards from the fort. He gave instructions to shoot it. That night a sentry fired.

In the morning there were marks of blood, but the track of the wounded animal could not be traced, as the ground was too hard. An old woman was found in the village wounded in the leg!

One encounter with hyenas gave me a far from pleasant thrill. I met a large male hyena not far from the banks of the Sissili river. He was coming towards me, evidently to drink, his nose uplifted above the rather tall grass. On either side of me was a man armed with an axe. The animal never saw me, but came steadily on, sniffing the air, but quite care-free. As it came on to a slight elevation

PLAYING AT WAR.

The arrows are fired in a crouching position by the Nankanni and other tribes. The men are throwing dust at the enemy as an insult.

CEREMONIAL SOWING.

Symbolic sowing by the Talansi in the ceremony of Korogu prior to more serious labour.

of the ground, about twenty yards from me, I fired and hit him well in the chest. He fell. The two men leapt at him. He got up and in his agony bit at his thigh where my bullet had made its exit. Then there ensued a great scuffle. The hyena and the two men revolved in an amazing mass. I could see fur and blood and black skins. The men shouted, the hyena made weird grunts and growls, and I screamed at the men to give me another shot. However the scrimmage did not last long. The hyena had revolved sufficiently backwards to its earth, and fell inside one of the entrances, leaving us three all agape at its marvellous escape.

No sound came from the earth. I knew the hyena had been mortally wounded, having been raked from chest to stern. We went and washed as much blood off ourselves as we could, and then proceeded on to my camp. It was too late to do anything that day, for the natives, naturally, would not care to dig up a hyena earth until they were certain the wounded animal was dead.

Next day was a Sunday, so I was free. I had sent, the previous evening, for men to meet me at the earth with hoes and other tools. As I left the camp my boy, Asutane, came and begged for permission to accompany me. There was no reason to refuse, so I consented. It took over an hour to reach the spot, and we had been some time there before the people arrived. They explained that they were late because they had had to make sacrifice—that a hyena which had behaved in so strange a fashion (my companions of the preceding day were their fellow-villagers, and had returned the previous night) was evidently more witch than animal; however, as I was a white man no doubt the magic (medicine) of my race would protect them, my servants.

I did my best to reassure them on this point, and we set to work. The outside of the earth was quite interesting. It had been constructed under an old weather-worn ant-heap, which makes a very hard soil, quite bare of growth. The hardness is due, I believe, to some chemical action or exudation from the termites. This old heap itself had been erected on the tumulus of some former compound, and lay in a thicket which included large trees of a growth subsequent to the abandonment of the village which had included this compound. It was a typical spot for such earths, which originally are always, I believe, constructed first by the aardvark or ant-eater, which is possibly ejected by the hyenas.

There were a number of holes visible, and tracks of recent use showed that there were several hyenas, inmates of the earth. We began work at the hole into which our hyena had disappeared. It smelt dreadfully. The sides of the tunnel were all covered with blood and hair, but no corpse was in sight. By the aid of long sticks we could trace the direction of these tunnels, and work began at various points. It was very tedious, and after close on two hours' hard effort we had not reached the body, and the only real progress made was that we had become quite certain that no living hyenas remained inside the earth.

My camp was in need of meat, so I wandered off alone to kill a kob, a herd of which I knew to be somewhere in the neighbourhood. It took me longer to locate than I had thought, and it was well over an hour before I returned to the earth. To my astonishment work had ceased, and before I had time to ask what was the reason I was told that the boy Asutane was calling for me; they could not understand him. (He was a Grunshi; they were Builsa.) I saw no boy. They informed me that he had gone into the earth to fetch out the body.

This startled me considerably. I went on to the tumulus and was shown a spot where I could hear the boy. My fears were great. I had visions of an earth fall, of all sorts of terrible possibilities; but when I put my ear to the ground I heard, seemingly a long way off, but quite clearly: "Massa, massa! send me some matches." To my questions the boy said he was all right, that he was unarmed, that he had found plenty of blood, and that he was not afraid of hyenas. I told him to come out, but he said he wanted only matches. I then explained to the people, and they sent a young man down with the matches and a spear. I waited on top in a state of fear mingled with anger.

Suddenly I heard Asutane's voice quite close to my feet. He said he was coming out. He emerged in a bramble cluster, together with the youth. I was too pleased to abuse him. He told me he had visited all the lairs of the hyenas, that one was very dark and even the matches could throw no light, and that he had had to come up as the smell was too great. He continued that he would not go in again on account of this smell. I told him he would not on any account.

When this story was told by me to some other natives, including a well-educated one, the latter said: "Oh yes! Asutane is not really a man-child at all. His father and his uncle are leopards and go into leopards' dens for the skins, which they sell in the market. And does not Asutane himself wander about alone at night unarmed and quite fearless? Why, the hyenas are his brothers, and they won't hurt him."

These stories show how easy it is to confuse animals or other things with that which one is thinking about, and how deeply lies this belief in wer-wolves. Every man who has hunted big game knows how frequently a rock or a tree can be mistaken at a casual glance for an expected animal, and how that rock or tree will quite easily and quickly be visualized into that animal, until every part of the beast is clearly visible. That peculiar delusion and the recurring series of coincidences help to foster, if not create, this belief in metamorphosis; and when, in addition, dreams are often considered as realities, what argument can possibly upset that belief?

Not every witch can change herself or himself into an animal. But it is worthy of note that, as in so many other parts of the world, the greater powers of magic and witch-craft are invariably attributed to the wilder and remoter tribes. Thus an Ashanti looks always on a Grunshi as a man "full of medicine," and to travel in Grunshi country —*i.e.* the northernmost parts of the Protectorate—is to enter into a land where disease and ill-fortune will be one's lot, unless one guards most carefully against these magic-sent misadventures.

Magic! In the ordinary way one thinks of something pleasant, surprising; but here it is the reverse. It is the most crushing form of discipline that the mind of man has ever created. Were it not for a few brave spirits who dare to risk disaster, no progress could be made. Imagine

—you who can afford to smile at these things—what life is like among the wilder and more savage of our hinterland people. Nothing can be done—not the most ordinary expedition to a neighbouring market—until omens have been taken and the augurs consulted. One cannot leave any of one's personal or intimate clothes, or one's hair or other part of one's body about, lest peradventure an enemy seize it and so work one mischief.

A man once came to me in the Zuaragu district. He had a complaint about someone having stolen away his wife from him. Customarily such a case is heard by the chief; and when I referred him to this native court he said: "Yes; that is so. But I cannot get to the chief's house." Pressed, he explained that his opponent's friends lived all around, and that he would have to pass close by their houses, and his footprint would be found by them. That meant that they could then gather up some of the dust crushed by his foot, which, impregnated as it was with his aura or personality, could be used to make charms over and so bewitch him that he might even die.

CHAPTER XII

ANIMAL CULTS

VOLUMES could be filled with instances we met with where magic played no small part. Space will permit of only a few being mentioned. One of the chief ideas behind this belief in magic is that a sort of spirit, aura, personality, exudes or exhales from the human body. Everything that belongs to the body, that has been in touch—even the slightest contact—with the body, or by natural process of reasoning anything resembling or made to resemble, can be made to represent that body. Thus a paring from a finger-nail, a portion of clothing, a foot-print, a figure moulded to resemble it, will play the rôle of the person to whom it belonged or resembled. And to so great an extent is this idea carried that even one's name is hidden lest by chance an enemy hearing it may work one ill.

Thus whenever one of these people enlists he never gives his real name. He is going away from his country, and if an enemy at home, who might know his name, used that name to magically work ill against him, the spirit of evil so invoked could not find him under his new name, by which alone his new comrades would know him.

In the north hair-clippings and nail-parings are not to-day so well looked after. Everyone knows it is risky to leave them about, but the superstition is certainly dying out. It can readily be understood that portions of the body more intimately connected with sexual matters are the most carefully guarded. Navel-strings, etc., are very, very well looked after.

The idea of a person passing by or coming in contact with anything saturating that thing with his personality is, so far as I have learned, universal throughout the country of which I write. Thus among the Konkomba I twice saw men sent down into the forest zone to bring back earth from the grave where one of the tribe had been buried, in order to carry out a proper funeral service and to rebury the man (*i.e.* earth impregnated with his personality) at home. Among the Builsa I met a case where the man's loin-cloth was buried instead of him. This they told me was unusual, as they would have preferred to have left him that, but he had no other clothing. This custom is, after all, not so very far from our own idea, so magniloquently expressed by Rupert Brooke:

> "If I should die, think only this of me:
> That there's some corner of a foreign field
> That is for ever England."

One of the most striking examples of this belief in the saturation (I lack a better word) of an object with the personality of the person or persons with whom it may come in contact is to be seen every day in Ashanti. No one who has visited that country can have failed to remark how whenever any Ashanti man or woman rises from his or her chair or stool, and is not going to reseat himself or herself almost at once, that chair or stool is reversed, and set either a-tilt against the wall or more often on its side. The reasons for this are, firstly, to prevent any wandering spirit sitting thereon, and so either take virtue from the rightful owner of the chair or leave an evil influence, a new saturation as it were, of something evil; and secondly, to prevent any stranger from sitting thereon with the same possible result. Shortly before Kojo died his dog, a puppy, actually ran through the people and sat on the stool of a chief who had just got up to address me. I am afraid my boy's death and that of his dog soon after were put down by the majority of the natives to that chief's magic power of avenging the insult.

In this connexion an interesting light may be shown by the following incident. When Kojo was still only a child I began to teach him to understand pictures. It must be remembered that a picture at first conveys nothing at all to the native mind, and one has to educate it painstakingly before it can grasp the meaning of a drawing—*i.e.* one of European effort. At last I got Kojo to recognize his Majesty the King and his two eldest sons. After that whenever a mail came in he extracted from me a promise to give him the pictures of our King. I did, and it amused me to watch the child go proudly to his friends and point out the King—upside down it nearly always used to be. But when, several years later, I had occasion to go into his room, where he was lying ill, to my astonishment the walls were all covered with those pictures of the King, the Prince of Wales and the Duke of York. I asked him why he kept them, since in his dark room one could not see them. And he answered: " Master, those are the pictures of the King and his children. No man must burn them or tear them, for the King and his children might die."

But if one cannot procure any article that has had actual contact with one's enemy, one can always fashion his form out of clay, and do evil to the image. In Ashanti I found amongst a collection of " medicines " taken from a " medicine-man " several interesting objects. One was a miniature bow and arrow used by the fellow to fire an arrow—an iron pin—into images thus made, and there where the arrow entered, disease and pain came to the unfortunate victim. There was also a small net all set about with bells. Its use was to ensnare the soul of any-one—or rather catch his aura, personality. But I never learned how one could make the aura or personality enter into a figure which had not come into contact with the person for whom it had to act as substitute.

The usual expression for illnesses thus caused is either " He was eaten by So-and-so " or, if only sickness ensued, " He has been tied by So-and-so." Time after time this is said to one. It accounts, undoubtedly, for the general idea that the Grunshi are cannibals, eaters of men—a statement one is always hearing on the coast. It really means that these wilder people are possessed with much magical power. That they have been cannibals in the past I am sure, just as in all probability at some distant date were the Ashanti, for until our final occupation there still existed the symbolic act of eating the hearts of important victims who were sacrificed. An old ex-executioner at Goaso told me that all the priests and other attendants touched with their lips, some even bit, the heart and kidneys of men so slain.

The "tying of men" is very common. I know of a certain quite well-educated man who, having passed over others senior to him in the service, naturally expected trouble. When he did fall sick, he told me that it was quite all right, that he knew who had "tied" him, and, knowing that, it was merely necessary for him to make a sacrifice or two and "counter-magic." But in the symbolic rite of tying, knots are actually made in a piece of string, which probably (I do not know for certain) has been properly dedicated for the purpose. At the same time the victim's name is mentioned, and at that precise moment he will fall ill.

If he does not, then it is evident that the intended victim is possessor of greater magic than his ill-wisher, against which reasoning no possible argument can prevail.

The practice of "tying" is used, however, not only for procuring ill. I have seen among various tribes the custom of tying grass alongside the paths. Several blades, still growing, are bent and knotted together. The explanation given is twofold. One is, that the owners of the growing crops have gone on a visit and they have tied the grass to prevent the goodness of their crops following them. The second is, to prevent any evil stranger taking away with him the goodness of those same crops. I have seen this practice regularly carried out over the whole of the hinterland visited by me.

Another common use of magic is to avert the "evil-eye" or to bring ill-luck by "overlooking." Throughout the Dagomba country, and all the territory under their influence, one will note at the corners of the various fields stones on which are black marks, crosses, circles, etc.

These are there to prevent evil ensuing from any remark a passer-by might make in praise of the crop. As in so many other places in the world, misfortune will surely follow such a statement as: " Why, that is a fine crop!"

For a similar reason it is discourteous to stand gazing at people eating. Even dogs must not do this, and if they do approach they are given scraps and driven away. Naturally to count one's property is sure to bring ill-luck. Did not rinderpest follow the cattle census? That it existed and was actually on our borders before then did not very much matter. It is, I think, a good thing that the terrible influenza epidemic did not come immediately after the 1921 general Census, which, of course, in any case was not—could not have been—accurate in detail, though by the law of averages it was probably nearly correct in sum-total.

A quite different series of beliefs is to be found in the use of charms, amulets, mascots, etc. The wearing or employment of these is to be found all through the country. I do not think that there need necessarily be much importance in these from a religious point of view, any more than our own practice of using mascots on motor-cars, aeroplanes, and in other matters, has any real effect on, or connexion with, Christianity.

There is, however, to be noted that many of the charms claim their power from having been in contact with some strength- or health-giving object. Thus a small piece of a lion's skin or, better, a portion of his heart, will obviously give its wearer and owner greater strength, better health and more bravery. A hair from an elephant's tail, which makes quite a neat armlet, is also quite evidently a good charm and mascot. So are leopards' claws or teeth, and so also are alleged copies of a few words from the Koran. Possibly there is also a trade in extracts from the Bible.

Other charms come from quite another source, and tend to become more than mascots, even to be abodes of guardian or well-wishing spirits. Such a one was a stone, a quite ordinary pebble, that an old orderly of mine picked up. He showed me it, and remarked that it was a fine stone, that he had never seen quite so curious a stone, and that he would keep it by him. Personally I could see nothing remarkable in the stone. It was merely a water-worn pebble, apparently of some quartz-like species. However, he took it back to our camp, and that same day learned that his wife had given birth to a boy-child. *Post hoc, propter hoc!* Several other bits of luck came his way shortly after. The stone's value grew, and its reputation became an important one. Two years later he left the force, time-expired. He was then sacrificing fowls to it.

Of course it is always magic of some sort that enables a man to get promotion or to bring off a successful business deal. This is easy to understand. For all men are the same. How then can one become a sergeant and another, recruited at the same time, remain a constable? Why is one thief taken and another not?

In this latter case the magical explanation will be that he failed to "tie" his victim. For it is the invariable practice of thieves throughout the country to be in possession of a magical tying apparatus—generally a donkey's tail. Before setting out on an expedition the name of the victim is spoken aloud and a knot is tied in the hairs of the tail, thus preventing him from waking or catching one.

The confirmed belief in all this magic has inevitably led to the rise of a class of men who act as consultants. I know of no Ashanti type of this character, but everywhere that the grass-zone people are, there one will find these consultants in numbers. At first one naturally presumes that such people would be of the charlatan variety, but I cannot believe that. The fees for a consultation are very small, and no consultant can refuse his help, no matter what may be his reputation; moreover, the consultants are as firmly convinced of the truth of this magic as are their clientele. It is curious how the Ashanti has escaped —or developed beyond—this stage of evolution.

So far as I have yet learned, it is possible for any man to become one of these consultants or soothsayers. (The actual word used throughout means "keeper of the bag.") Such a career is determined for one either by one's parents or by some series of events which has led one, oneself, to consider that one's duty is to become a "keeper of the bag." A short apprenticeship is served with an older and experienced "keeper," and in course of time one passes various tests of magic and divination, and, as it were, receives a degree in the Black Art, which entitles one to practise. There is no hardship in this; details are not necessary, as the process is an ordinary one of learning and rather commonplace. Suffice it to say that, apart from the extraordinary results in reasoning that one obtains from the false association of ideas, there is absolutely nothing of mystery or conjuring or any wonderful thing at all.

French writers who deal with this type of soothsayer call them " relaters of hidden things "; and the natives, as above remarked, " keepers of the bag." Those two expressions convey at one and the same time the duty and the manner of acting of these men.

Now in every single little everyday affair a Northern Territory man will consult one of these " keepers of the bag," if he has the time. " Shall I hoe over my guinea-corn to-morrow?" " Shall I go hunting?" " Will to-morrow be a good day to heap up the ground-nuts?" " What day shall I go to visit Awuni?" " Is Tamputi my friend?" " Shall I get a good exchange for my goat at the market to-morrow?" Or the more serious questions: " Why has my child died?" " What has caused the blight on my millet?" " Why are my yams drying up?"

These questions are obvious ones to take before a " keeper of the bag." So one pays him a visit. This would generally be in the evening, but any time will do. After the usual greetings one tells him that one desires to consult " the bag."

This he fetches. It is usually a goatskin or sheepskin pulled over the animal's tail and not slit down the stomach. Inside are a number of all sorts of articles, collected at various times for various reasons—stones, old bones, old horns, bits of tin or iron, a bead or two, and one or two cowries. These are spread about on the ground, and the consultant and his client squat down with this weird collection between them. The " keeper " has in his right hand a stick—the magic wand—and in his left a gourd, in which seeds or little stones have been placed, so that it has become quite a rattle.

Now the client either tells his trouble to the "keeper of the bag" or not. The procedure is the same. Let us suppose that in this case he does not, and let us take the question: "Shall I hoe over my guinea-corn to-morrow?" The answer is certainly either "Yes," "No," or "Wait for another day."

The client takes three of the articles—in this case probably the stones, as no other exhibit would be more appropriate or in closer magical sympathy with the field. He sets them apart and, picking them up one by one, whispers to each in turn the answer "Yes" or "No," etc. Thus each stone to his mind indicates a separate answer. All this time the "keeper of the bag" has been shaking his rattle and calling to the "little men" (I refer to these later) to go away. As soon as the client has told the stones for what answer they are standing he takes in his right hand the other end of the magic wand which is held by the "keeper of the bag." The latter mutters his magic formulæ (these I have never learned) and gradually moves the wand over and around the stones. The client uses no force, but lets his hand be guided by the "keeper of the bag." Nearer and nearer to the stones comes the wand, until at last one of the stones is touched, then hit. That is the answer wanted. A second and a third time is this done; and nearly always the same stone, or rather the same answer, is obtained.

There is no mystery here. The client in reality has already subconsciously made up his mind, and the answering muscular reaction has, unwittingly to him, caused his end of the wand to touch that stone to which that decision had been conveyed.

So it is with the graver question of: " How (or why) did my child die? " The answer to that might be one or more of several: the client may not have sacrificed to any one of the scores of spirits; his ancestors may have been neglected; witches may have bewitched the child; and so on.

Then more stones and articles from the bag are selected. But the procedure is the same, as it is if one tells the " keeper of the bag." For he will then tell the articles from his bag what each is to represent. His greater knowledge of matters magical will thus be brought into service.

I mentioned above " the little men." All over the hinterland and in the forest zone the belief in the existence of dwarfs, elves, pixie-folk—call them what you will—is to be found. These are sometimes visible, but more usually not. They are shaped like human beings and have all the attributes of man. They are pre-eminently mischief-workers, and are said to " throw stones at one as one passes through the bush." That expression I have never fathomed. It is implicitly believed in. Moreover, these little men are blamed frequently for unexpected births: they " change " children; they make them crazy or deformed. In Ashanti they are called *mmotia*, in the Northern Protectorate they are *chichiriga*; or dialect varieties of that term.

It is not possible in a volume such as this to give a thorough account of the religion of these people. I have merely outlined it. But it is very necessary to mention another belief which is general and somewhat akin to totemism.

I have found no trace of any family asserting that their ancestor was an animal; but it is occasionally found that an animal is adopted as a man's *alter ego*. For instance, the appearance of an unusual animal, or an unexpected event concerning an animal, might coincide with a man's birth or his death. Such an animal or plant would quite likely be taken as a "brother," and in some mystic fashion be held to be his *alter ego*, or again, in some equally mystic way, be so closely connected with him that he and the animal merge their respective identities the one into the other.

But one finds very frequently and generally throughout the country an animal looked upon as a member of the family because of some event in the past history of that family in which the animal came to the aid or rescue of that family's ancestors. Thus it is that the crocodile is often taken as the animal brother. Tradition is remarkably similar, not only in families but also in tribes and nations, and the crocodile is one of the commonest of animals to have befriended man. I have found him protected for past services among the Dagomba, Konkomba, Kassena, Mamprussi and Dagati. Possibly in every tribe one might find this tradition.

One might here observe that the cult of the crocodile, whether it be of totemic origin or not, is by far the commonest of animal cults in the Protectorate. The main points in the religion of the people is the same everywhere, as I have endeavoured to point out, and varies only in the details. But here one has an outside practice almost equally widely distributed. To a certain degree, in a country where watercourses are numerous and crocodiles are to be found in even the smallest of streams and ponds, it might naturally be expected that the people dwelling in close proximity to an animal capable of becoming dangerous would tend to respect that animal, and in return that animal, realizing that he had nothing to fear from them, would leave them alone. Thus a child would be taught to let sleeping dogs lie. In course of time the dog's children would also learn that the man-child would not harm him. A mutual understanding would ensue, and in the gradual process of time would receive a semi-theological explanation, especially as stranger crocodiles would not possibly know of its existence. Of course this is just surmise. But so common is this worship of the crocodile, or rather respect paid to it, that if ever one wanted to choose an emblem symbolic of these people, grouped as one, nothing could be more apt than a representation of this saurian.

Again, a possible explanation which shows reason for the respect or gratitude for past services is to be found in the false logic of the native which almost invariably confuses cause and effect. In a country such as this, where drought is far from rare and into which most of the people have migrated from the drier lands of the north, the question of a good water-supply is of paramount importance, and a new settler's first duty would naturally be to see that it was secured. The presence of crocodiles in a pool or pond, or their tracks across the mud or sand, would tell him that water was there. He would also know that when the crocodiles left the watering-place then the water would be finished. He therefore argued that the presence of the crocodile accounted for the presence of the water, and was therefore correspondingly grateful.

In process of time he would, by the very force of his observation of coincidences, and through the medium of the same fallacious logic, argue and come to believe that the birth of baby crocodiles coincided with the birth of his own babies and that they died at the same time as men. Thus they would correspond in their lives, and so the entire belief in their being an *alter ego* would arise.

But, as I have said before, all this is surmise and theory. It cannot be proved and the native is never likely now to be able to give us the true explanation. The only use in such surmises as these, drawn from only a very, very few observations, and therefore of extremely small value, is to show a process of thought which, if not absolutely true in this case, is at least commonly found among these people.

M. Delafosse says on this subject, in an article which appeared in *La Revue d'Ethnographie*, Part II.: "The explanation which all the natives of West Africa give for it [*i.e.* belief in some family tie with an animal] is that the ancestor of the human group had been saved from death or some perilous situation by a member of the species or category, and in gratitude had consecrated it for himself and all his future descendants and had consigned to evil each of these latter who might in some way or other harm some one of the beings of this species or some object in that category. Be the explanation true or false, transmitted by tradition or invented for the need of its explanation, it matters little; the fact that it is spontaneously offered by all the inhabitants of West Africa should suffice to prove that it accords well with the conception that they hold of the matter."

CHAPTER XIII

FORBIDDEN ACTS

A LOGICAL outcome of the animal cult is a long list of forbidden acts. These are ordinarily called taboos; but since the use of a foreign word is thereby again brought about, I will endeavour to avoid using it.

The list of forbidden acts is immense and varied. It does not serve much purpose in a general work to quote them at any length. They are of the usual sort. Prohibitions to kill certain animals or to partake of their meat; reservations of rivers and pools; hunting restrictions; rules for the use of water and regulations concerning the planting or harvesting of crops. Arguing from our point of view one is inclined to explain these materialistically. One can easily understand that the preservation of fish requires the prohibition of fishing in certain places or at certain seasons. But it is not possible to say that therein is the real cause. Here, as elsewhere in the realm bordering on religious thought, one is at a loss to draw exact conclusions on account of the complete absence of doctrine or any reliable record. One generally finds, however, that all these rules are beneficial in the long run to the family or community, and whether they have arisen haphazardly or intentionally will probably remain for all time unsolved. The native does not require any deep reason for them. Like all agriculturists he is content to follow the habits and customs observed by his forbears, and leaves explanations to others. One cannot blame him for this, since we are almost as bad as he.

I have endeavoured already to point out how all matters are really settled for the individual after inquiry is made from the "keeper of the bag." In this way one would find out what animal is particularly beneficial or friendly inclined to one's child; and, as the subconscious mind of the consultant at all these inquiries is the real solving factor, it stands to reason that the animal longest treated or regarded as such by the family stands the greatest chance of being selected for the newly born member of that family.

In this way is perpetuated the respect or cult of certain animals, and of course in process of time one need scarcely trouble to consult the "keeper of the bag," unless to ascertain if a second animal should be taken into regard as well. This one finds not infrequently to be the case.

This practice continued for some time would inevitably lead to a multiplicity of animals or plants reverenced by a family or tribal group. We find that this is so among these people. Thus at Paga, in the Kassena country, the crocodiles of a large pool are looked upon as being the *alter ego* of the members of one family to such an extent that it is said that for every member of that group there is a crocodile, and that this animal is born and dies at the same time as his corresponding human, and suffers with him from griefs and pains and sickness. No stranger who lives or is born at Paga has a crocodile equivalent, however. Now the people of Paga have also quite a lot of other animals which they regard similarly, though not to the same extent. These vary in each family and among the members of each family. They may have been determined by an ancestor later than the first or may have been merely allotted to the individual by the "keeper of the bag." Or again, some circumstance during the lifetime of the individual may have caused him to conclude that an animal or a plant has become particularly friendly disposed towards him.

This practice of maintaining respect for an animal or plant or some custom is frequently the origin of family names. It is usual for every native to have such a family name, but he seems particularly chary of publishing it. Ordinarily they will not tell it us at all. Possibly it is forbidden to mention it. In any case it usually exists. Here one meets with that contrast in thought so common among primitive people. The name might just as easily be taken from an animal which has been traditionally hostile to the family as from one that has been friendly. Such names are often contracted phrases reminding their bearers of some event in the past history of the family, and have nothing to do with the animals respected. That is another question, however, and no longer concerns religion.

It must be remembered that the native, however, does not look upon these animals, etc., as creating any relationship except in his immediate family. Thus a crocodile Dagomba is no relation to a Kassena crocodile. I have not learned whether a Kassena crocodile-man can kill a crocodile in Dagomba, but I am inclined to think he could, as one generally finds that the river crocodiles are not at all sacred to the men who claim relationship with those of pools. He would, however, not eat the meat of the animal. One notices this often out hunting, and meat is declined if the animal is sacred to the man.

Whenever a stranger enters a compound at the time of the evening meal he is invited to partake of the repast. The stranger will usually accept. He will be anxious to know the contents of the dishes spread before him; and if he suspects the food is of meat forbidden to him he will not be at all shy in inquiring what there is in the dishes, nor does anyone think it wrong if he declines for religious reasons. I asked what happens when the answer given is a lie. This is not infrequent among the Nankanni, and they see a certain humour in making a man eat his forbidden dishes. The answer given me was that the man was innocent of any intent and was merely misled. No harm would come to him. And as the Nankanni fear not at all the protecting deities of other tribes they also get off scot-free from this practical joke. Other tribes are not quite so careless of other people's gods and do not jest in these matters.

SECRET SOCIETY DANCES.

The young men of the Bimoba belonging to the Konne Society dance in this peculiar crouching attitude.

CHAPTER XIV

CEREMONIAL DANCING

ONE very little-studied side of the religion of the natives is their ceremonial dancing. It is not often that a European is able to witness such dances. I myself in Ashanti saw the Dance of Inspiration, which the village priest went through before he became, as it were, possessed by the very spirit of his god; I have seen the symbolic seed-time festival of the Talansi; and I watched ceremonial religious dancing of a secret society among the Bimoba.

It was at Goaso that I saw the first-mentioned. I had been asked to give permission for the dance, and having, as we always do, given assent, myself went to watch. It took place at about ten o'clock in the morning. I arrived at the place—the village street—somewhat late. Drumming had already begun, and the brass basin, in which was lying hidden, under many rags and cloths, the article (I never saw what it was or what it was made of) in which the god or spirit usually dwelt, was held by a small boy. The village priest, a young man who was a good friend of mine, as he was an excellent hunter, was almost naked, having only a grass kilt on and some amulets tied under his knees and on his wrists. He seemed to be in a kind of stupor; his eyes were somewhat vacant, his whole bearing far from natural. From time to time he shook hands or touched people as he wandered about the crowd. The drumming grew louder and quicker. The priest began to dance. Two attendants with cow-tails kept back the crowd. Quicker and quicker beat the drums: the priest leapt and danced. An attendant sprinkled him with a white powdered clay; the sweat made it run in streaks down his body and over his face. Soon his torso and face were all white. But the dance waxed ever fiercer and wilder. Presently the boy who bore the basin entered the ring and, with the help of the two attendants, placed it on the head of the priest, who leapt more and more frantically. The drums were by this time being beaten louder than ever: an atmosphere of expectant excitement pervaded the crowd. Presently the priest began to quiver all over. The muscles of his back and chest, and the calves of his legs, all began to vibrate. Sweat poured off him, and clouds of powder were thrown at him. Gradually he drew back and slackened the pace of his dance, but his quakings grew more violent. The attendants could hardly keep the basin on his head. At last he reached a stool, kept for him, and subsided. The spirit of the god had entered him, and he was now prepared to talk; but first the mothers took their babies to him, all awed into unwonted silence. These he touched, whilst the mothers bowed reverently before him. I did not watch any longer.

The second ceremonial dance that I witnessed was at Tongo, in the Nankanni country. Another European was with me, and it was quite by accident that we stumbled across this interesting ceremony. It was in March, the last month of the dry season; two or three showers had fallen, and it is the usual practice to start one's planting after the third or fourth rain.

Our attention was drawn to the fact that there was something unusual afoot by observing the young women. They go about naked in this part, wearing only a bunch of leaves fore and aft. This day they were well oiled, with their heads newly shaved, and they had great necklaces and girdles of beads instead of the leaves.

On inquiry we learned that there was a big dance on that evening. We attended. The chief's " son " acted as our guide and explained as much as he could. It was a very striking affair. The dance had already begun when we arrived on the scene. Except for the noise of the shuffling feet there was no sound, no drumming. Very few onlookers were present, all were partaking in the ceremony.

The people were dancing in one long file, following the movements of a young man, who wound his file into a tight circle, like the spring of a clock, and then unwound them. All in silence. But the stamping and dancing, the shuffle forward, then back, were all carried out strenuously. As the group unwound itself the men received from children standing by swords, bayonets, knives and knob-kerries. These were brandished, and again a circle was made. This was repeated several times, till the dust nearly overcame us.

At last the dancers moved away to the foot of the hills and there made a large circle, with a cleared space in the middle. Into this danced three men—one a very old one. Suddenly one of them began to sing, and the dancers, who were all the time on the move, answered him with a "M-m-m-m," quite well intoned. Our interpreter told us that presently the three men would scatter some millet grains and then finish the dance, after which the people would rush to get at least one grain each, for that would bring good luck to their crops that year. Afterwards ordinary dancing would take place and every-one would give themselves up to playing and singing and otherwise enjoying themselves.

Unfortunately we did not see the end. The dancing stopped, and our interpreter told us that the old men were afraid to go on in our presence, as they had never heard of such a thing as Europeans attending such an important ceremony. There was no fear at all of anything illegal taking place, so we said we would leave them alone to carry on, and would hope to see the end another year.

My third experience of a really ceremonious dance was in the Bimoba country, a small area in the extreme north of the old German colony of Togoland. The following account I wrote for *The Journal of the African Society*.

"I had been coming through the bush, and as I was riding quietly along the path there came along a party of five men clad only in cowrie-bedecked strips of cloth—a striking sight, since all men here are clothed usually in native jumpers or at least drawers. When they reached me they bent to the ground and danced past, crouch-ing and greeting me with a low guttural growl. This naturally roused my curiosity, and one of the sons of the chief of Solotigu provided me with the following information:—

"'These men are members of a secret society which is to be found in most villages. The society is entirely of

Bimoba origin, members of which are known as Konne (*pl.* Konse). After reaching puberty all young men are eligible. They are taken to an old man, owner of the society's *bari* or medicine, and therefore local head of the Konse. After three days their entry is approved, and a house of grass mats is erected for them near the Lari's (head of the Konse) compound. Here the candidate remains secluded for four months. He is taken there at night, and no man may see his going. He may not come out till the period of seclusion is past, and his wants are attended to by a boy and girl, who are named his father and mother. The owner of the *bari* renames them, and by these names only may they be known after their re-entrance into society. To mention their original name is death from sickness in a short time. These Konse names are: Lari, Sangso, Duti, Kombete, Lolaa, Lamboa, Sambeg, Samwog, Bonbog. They learn a special language unintelligible to the uninitiated. It is certainly a weird language, sounding like so many growls, but when sung in chorus is of an extraordinarily pleasant hearing.

"'They learn, too, a series of dances and the strange manner of walking first noticed by me—crouching towards the ground and skipping or dancing rather than walking along. And they learn to use their left hand with which to eat meat and not, as is customary, the right. This is during the probationary period of four months. But even more interesting than this subversion of custom is the fact that, except for meat, they may use no hands at all for eating. Their "mother" feeds them. The food is usually millet or guinea-corn porridge soaked in water. She ladles the food out with a calabash, which she holds to their lips. Goat-flesh and fish are forbidden during this time.'

" If a Kussasi youth wishes to become a member he has to undergo a rather frightening ordeal. He is cut with a knife and medicine is inserted in the wounds; thereby he is reduced to unconsciousness for a long time. 'He dies for five days' is the expression used. They then anoint him with other medicine, and he returns to consciousness.

" When the four months' seclusion is completed the father of the candidate provides a feast for him and his 'father and mother' attendants, and gives to the Lari three fowls, four hundred cowries, four pots of native beer, four calabashes of food and three pots of cooked meat. During the ensuing month—the first after their liberation—they give themselves up to dancing and feasting. They are terribly excited at this time and cannot remain at rest. I saw one outside the chief of Solotigu's compound, and he was ever on the move and looked like one half-crazed."

The season for the initiation period is naturally the dry season, lest farming should suffer, and I was fortunate enough to be at Solotigu just after the seclusion period had ended and during the month of festivity. The chief gave me the pleasure of witnessing a dance. We first had to hold a political palaver and the dancers were very restless. One fainted from excitement—a not unusual event among these savages.

Freed from duty, we adjourned to the shade of a locust-bean-tree, and the dance began.

There were fourteen dancers, attended by their late "mothers." They were covered with cowries: they had a band of these shells round the forehead; several thick necklaces, some hanging well below the waist; five bands of cowries girdled their loins, and tucked in behind was the skin of an oribi with the hair side showing, whilst in front was a small blue loin-cloth almost covered with strings of cowries, which hung from ropes of the same shell that encircled the neck. Each, too, had a leather bag decorated with the same shell hanging in front. Wristlets and armlets were of the same design, and anklets and bands round the top of the knees were of iron. On either arm above the elbow was a wooden ring, and on the ankles were iron bangles hung about with loose iron rings, which rattled as they danced. In addition every dancer wore necklaces of beads of European manufacture.

On the left shoulder they all carried axes and in their right hands a horse-tail, of which the handle was studded with the shells. The left hand grasped the axe-handle, and was armed with a dagger, of which the hilt passed over the palm and was still further guarded by being tied with a leather thong to the leather wrist-shields which every bowman must wear; on the right hand was a sharply pointed knuckle-duster and an iron ring on the thumb. Earrings of iron and a necklace of threaded iron rings completed the dress, the back being crossed with cowrie bands. The *tout ensemble* was not only strikingly picturesque but extraordinarily attractive.

Music for the dance was supplied by drummers, who were clothed ordinarily. The drums resemble roughly trimmed side-drums, and were painted red, white and black in stripes. They all showed traces of sacrifices to them, blood and feathers remaining stuck on their sides.

The dance was accompanied by a song in the guttural growling speech of the society. So far as I could make out the steps were not intricate, but the time was excellent—a short step forward with the left foot, the right one then came to its heel; a second short step with the left, the dancer then leapt about a yard on the left; the right foot came up, and a third short step with the left. When the dance ceased, each covered his features with the horse-tail and his attendant "mother" wiped the sweat from his brow with her hand.

A second dance followed. Each gave up his horse-tail and took a drawn sword of native manufacture. The scabbard was slung on the left hip. I could not make out the step. From time to time the sword was thrust into the sand and the dancer bent over it, all the time chanting in their guttural tones. They suddenly massed together with sword-points on the ground and bodies bent bowed before me. I was told they were saluting me and asking leave to go. They sang a chant, almost Gregorian, whilst awaiting my dismissal. I was nearly tempted not to let them go, but had pity on them, for the sun was high and the heat intense.

BUILSA DANCES.

Out of deference to the Author, the men clothed themselves. Ordinarily they dance naked. In the top illustration one man is seen pulling on his trousers, which are of native woven cloth.

CHAPTER XV

THE LOVE OF DANCING

IT is often alleged that dancing is in its origin religious or ceremonial. That is to me a very debatable point. I am rather inclined to believe that dancing is a spontaneous expression on the part of a body of people of contentment and joy. One lives out here in closer contact with natural man than at home, and one is naturally bound to observe customs and habits more nearly. So-called savage man laughs aloud with joy; so-called civilized man only does so while he is still in the cradle. We mask our feelings. If one kills a large animal here, one's carriers know they will have plenty of "meat." They laugh aloud. I do not think diners at the Ritz do that when first they glance at the menu. It is the same with dancing.

Natives are nearly always ready to dance; but there is no question of "nearly" when a real occasion is offered. One sees this particularly with one's carriers. Thoroughly tired after a long day, they will not dance under ordinary circumstances; but they cannot resist it when there is some really good thing to celebrate.

In every tribe there are set dances as well as impromptu ones. The former tend to become almost ceremonial. Thus one finds hunting dances, funeral dances, market-day dances—in which everyone takes part; favourite tunes are played and well-known songs are sung, for dancing and singing almost always go together.

It is also more or less general for dancing to take place in the evening, which is quite natural, seeing that one's daily work is not thereby interfered with. But funeral-custom dances or wakes are often daylight entertainments. Missionaries endeavour to put an end to this dancing, as they allege that it leads to immorality. Possibly they are right. But what a pity if, because of the straying of the few, the whole nation should be punished, and in the event of this country becoming Christian all these happy folk-songs and folk-dances were to be lost! Personally the old-time counsels of St Gregory and St Augustine seem to me the best—"Destroy not, but rather bend the pagan customs and usages to the service of God." This is controversial, and into the sphere of controversy I will not enter.

Native dances are at first sight quite interesting because of their unfamiliarity and quaintness. But I think most of us grow weary of their sameness. Africa is the home of all the jazz and other modern dances of Europe, with the sole difference that instead of having partners one dances solo but together with a number of others. A circle is formed, two or three drummers stand in the middle, tom-tomming begins, and the dancers line up in an endless queue, shuffle and walk, turn and twist—a "follow-my-leader" sort of affair. Individuals often make their own variations, following apparently their own whims. That is the usual dance.

I think dancing must be like music—understandable only by the few. For to me there seems but little amusement, little pleasure in the performance. Each tribe has of course its own favourite folk-dances. There is the "sibi-saba"—a jazz, as we corruptly call it—of the Twi speakers; the muscle-shaking dance of the men of the north; and the stern-bumping women's dance of the Dagomba. This last is quite striking. Two groups of women are formed: they dance and clap their hands; then two dance into the centre, turn about back to back, and suddenly leaping into the air, bring their sterns into violent collision; then dancing back to their group they are met with outstretched hands, when the dancers place their palms into the palms of their *vis-à-vis*, leap into the air and resume their position in the group.

There are some dances in the north that are really good "shows," especially those of the Talansi, where the dancing is carried out by well-drilled companies, who sing quite stirring songs while they dance, keeping step magnificently, and from time to time bringing their feet down with a stamp that shakes the earth. I think such dances are probably those of secret societies, though I do not know for certain.

But the finest effect and the wildest is when one can witness a dance not by moonlight but by torchlight. The flare of the torches, the falling sparks, the black skins glistening with sweat, the dancing, the wild guttural singing and the maddening tom-tomming cause a wonderful effect of wildness and savagery, which is now fast disappearing.

And as the evening wears on the dancers grow happier and happier, apparently never getting tired. Then it is that, however often I have seen these things, I love to go to watch. There, during a halt of the general dance, two or three of the girls will enter the circle and give an exhibition. A lover or an admirer steps out and places on their gleaming shoulders a handkerchief or some such token of his admiration, or a drummer for a moment ceases to drum and places his drumstick, shaped like a hook, on the favoured one's shoulder—only for a moment however—then he steps back and again drums madly but rhythmically.

Among the Konkomba there is a notable dance which I think is in reality a pure ceremonial one. This is the Fire Dance. It takes place usually at the beginning of November and is a wild enough affair to satisfy most people. Great torches are lit, the people dance naked, and to snuff the torches hit each other with the flaming brands. In my opinion this dance is the celebration of harvest-home and the signal that the season for burning the bush has arrived.

In the northern portions of the Protectorate there is a play-dance held at the big funeral wakes, which usually take place a year after the burial, but are invariably timed for the dry season. Relations and friends of the deceased assemble in great numbers at his late home, and general feasting and play are indulged in. The young men arrange an attack on this home, and in full war-apparel, decorated with helmets made of gourds or woven rope all covered with cowries or skins of monkeys and leopards, with horns of antelopes set in them, and carrying beautifully adorned quivers full of arrows, their bows in their hands, they advance in mimic warfare against the house. War-cries and shouts are raised: all the tactics of real battle are indulged in, short of firing the arrows, until at last the house is reached, when they all shout the shout of victory, assemble together, and sing and dance to the older relatives, who await them with guinea-corn, beer and other refreshments.

A very interesting type of dancing is one not far removed from play-acting. I was once at a village called Nabune, in the Konkomba country. About four in the afternoon I was disturbed by the drumming of dancers approaching the rest-house. I watched them advance towards me. Two men were crouching in front of the band, one robed in a lion's skin and one armed with bow and arrows. It was quite evident what the play meant. A lion was being hunted. This continued for some time. The "lion" at times ran away and was stalked by the hunter. The former roared and the latter made believe to shoot. At last they came quite close to the rest-house compound, and there the "lion" lay down and "died," and the hunter removed the pelt. This same hunter had recently killed a lion, and by means of this play, with the villagers as a dancing and drumming chorus, he showed me and all what he had accomplished. Everyone enjoyed the little scene, and laughed and applauded the antics of the "lion" and the prowess of the hunter.

Often one comes across this form of embryonic drama. At a place called Sambruno, in the Nankanni country, there dwelt a comedian. He had two set pieces which always were received with acclamation and delight by his fellow-villagers. This man had a habit of coming down the road to meet one. He was more or less naked, his body being bedecked however with necklets of string, to which oddments, such as portions of old clock wheels, a tin-opener, various charms, etc., were attached; armlets and anklets equally curious, and an old rag of a loin-cloth. On his head was a straw hat—such a hat! It was dirty and old, torn and full of holes, bedaubed with mud and blood and feathers, had a very wide brim, and the crown was adorned with brown-and-white wing-feathers of a chicken-hawk.

He held in his hands a long stalk of guinea-corn, to one end of which was tied a blood-encrusted bunch of fowls' feathers. As he approached me he drew aside, and, placing the stalk between his legs, with the feathers in front, made believe it was a horse, and prancing and kicking he imitated a rider on a fiery steed all the way to the rest-house, when he would "dismount" and make believe to feed and water his courser. The crowd enjoyed this, and one usually rewarded his absurdities with a coin. This bought him a fowl or two, and when he ate them he never forgot to reward his "steed," the instrument by which he had earned them, by giving it some blood and feathers. It is a universal practice thus to reward such instruments: the drums, the "violins," one's agricultural tools, the smithy's furnace, etc., are always given blood and feathers.

His second piece was given at the end of the "palaver," or pow-wow, which one held with the assembled people. For this he had an assistant. The two of them pretended to go hunting, and went through all the motions of stalking the animal. At last he considered he was near enough to hazard a shot. Then carefully and with much parade of stealthiness he would wad his gun (a hollowed-out bamboo stalk), add powder (dust from the road) and, drawing close to the imagined quarry, would aim, and suddenly blowing out the dust, as if firing the "gun," he would pretend to miss, thus giving him an opportunity to repeat the play-acting.

CHAPTER XVI

GAMES

"MAKE-BELIEVE" games are common among the children of all the tribes with whom I have come in contact. From the very first they seem to love to imitate their elders, and the latter naturally do not fail to encourage this pathetic keenness to hurry into adultdom. As if they did not have to work enough later on! One will see little tots carrying minute pots full of water on their heads; and small boys have their own little plots of land which they more or less cultivate. But such games partake of the nature of real work and are serious.

Other games are played in lighter mood. In the chapter on religion I recounted how the village priest danced and received into his body the spirit of the local god. A few days after that incident I came across some children playing they were awaiting the coming of the spirit. There were the "priest," his two attendants, and an old enamel basin to hold the "god's" spirit. The "priest" made his muscles quiver and shake, and his attendants covered his sweating body with powdered clay. Unfortunately the children saw me and ran away.

Once in the Konkomba country I had had my tent pitched in the shade of a tree just outside a compound. I was supposed to be dozing after lunch. A small boy and a small girl came out. They pretended that one

TALANSI WOMEN,

dressed for very important occasions, usually they wear a bunch of leaves back and front. Glass beads are round their necks and are very heavy.

IN SUNDAY BEST.

A youth dressed for market. A whistle hangs from his neck, and round his forehead is a band of white and red beads.

was a horse and the other the groom. The horse was in imagination " tethered." It was fed and watered and groomed. Then it broke its imaginary tethering rope, was caught and retied. It kicked its groom. Result—tears and howls. The father came out, smacked the " groom " and whipped the " horse." More tears and more howls. But as there was no further appearance of the elder folk, the two children wandered off outside my vision.

But the best " make-believe " play I came across was at Goaso. The village chief had bought two kegs of black powder, which he intended to keep for a funeral custom that was due to take place a month or two later. (These customs or wakes are not held at the time of the burial, for obvious reasons.) Now he had a son who was the leader of a large gang of the village boys. The youngster knew where the kegs had been hidden, so he organized his gang into a hunting party. They made a gun out of a leg-bone of a sheep, hollowing it out almost as far as the knuckle. A touch-hole was then bored, and a ready-made pistol resulted. He then " borrowed " some powder, and every day the gang went into the forest, where they made a camp. Their kill—for the toy pistol was quite a workmanlike article—consisted of mice and lizards and other small " meat." They had a fire, cooked their game, and had quite a good time until the first keg was nearly empty. Then it was that the chief found out, with the result that everyone got whipped and put on short rations for a time.

In the grass country the boys go out every morning during the dry season with the cattle. This gives them a very fine opportunity to play, and they organize wars and battles. Each boy is given some roasted ground-nuts for lunch by his family. These are all pooled and the winning gang eats the lot. Fights such as these are quite bloodthirsty affairs; knob-kerries and sticks are used, and often heads are cracked. This is doubly unfortunate to the sufferer, for not only has he got a cracked skull, but he bears on him the proof that he has been fighting and usually receives chastisement at home as well.

The similarity between games such as the above and our own childish ones is very striking. European influence is also everywhere apparent. Even in the remotest villages one will see a wheel, made of the bottom of some discarded tin, attached to a handle-bar; hoops are common, but not, however, always quite circular. Then golf and football are imitated, the former being adapted to a team game and becoming somewhat like hockey without goals, while the principal aim is to see how long one can keep possession of the ball (a stone).

Girls have dolls—weird little wooden images, with sexual distinctions prominently displayed. They are dyed black too! Their hair is of prickly spines, so that the head is somewhat like a black pincushion. Their "mothers" clothe them or give them girdles and necklaces of beads or other ornaments, and carry their "offspring" on their backs. Playing at "mother" is just as prevalent here as at home. I have a curious doll from Dagomba country, an old smoke-stained bone, with a rag for a dress, and some cowries and a coin (one-tenth of a penny—a nickel coin pierced in the centre for stringing) as a necklace. These dolls have frequently been mistaken for idols.

In Ashanti the boys have some very ingenious games

which are played in company. One or two of them I shall describe, for these, simple though they be, are fast disappearing. The demand for labour in the cocoa orchards and fields requires the help of most children, and the missionaries, since the war, have made great progress, almost inconceivable progress, in that country, and they do not countenance these gatherings of the young. But it has always been the custom for the old men of the village to forbid a game, however innocent, as soon as ever it has become really popular. This in itself may seem harsh, but I think there is a certain amount of wisdom in it, for discipline and self-restraint are thereby inculcated.

The boys divide themselves into two parties and go outside the village to a wider clearing on one of the paths. They make a missile of an old corn-cob wrapped in leaves all carefully tied together. This somewhat resembles a shuttlecock, having one end, where the cob is, heavier than the other. It is then thrown over a rope, made of a creeper, tied across the path about eight feet high. Each player has as a racket (!) a running noose made of a very strong, almost wire-like liane. The game is to catch the cob when thrown over the rope with this noose before it touches the ground. When seven have been caught by one side a victory is gained.

Another game played in the village street requires merely a noose of fine twine (a strand of piassava will do) and some sand. This latter is heaped up and one of the players buries the noose under the heaped-up sand. Then each player in turn takes a small stick—a thorn from a lime-tree is usual—and sticks it into the heap of sand where he expects the noose to be, the hider being the last to play. The end of the string is then uncovered and pulled, and if a thorn is inside the noose, that thorn's player wins.

Yet another game is played with small stones. Each player squats on the ground with six pebbles in front of him. The leader gives the word, and each player, with his right hand only or his left only, according to the leader's command, picks up stone by stone, throws each into the air and catches it. No stones may be dropped. When all are finished the stones are put on the ground again and two of them at a time are so treated, then three at a time, then four and two, then five and one, then six altogether. The one who finishes first must then rapidly shout out: "*Fo*, *Nwuna*, *Nkyi*, *Kuru*, *Mono*," and he wins.

Now in all these games the losers must pay forfeit. This is invariably some corporal punishment or other. For instance in the battledore and shuttlecock game each of the winning side gives each of the losers a blow with a stick; in "pricking the noose" the hider, if the noose is pricked, holds out his arm and receives on it a blow from the hand of each player; if no one finds the noose and he does, he is entitled to throw a lime at each of the others (I should hate this if I were a boy). In the stone-catching game the winner gives each of his opponents one. But if he forgets the magic formula at the end he is pelted with limes by the others.

That formula is interesting. It would seem that the words mean one, two, three, four, five. But they are not the numerals of the modern language. Maybe they are survivals of a forgotten tongue, just as are "eena, meena, mina, mo," or "hickory, dickory, dok" of our own nursery rhyme. However it may be, those words are prefixes used in the Ashanti calendar—a discovery first disclosed, I believe, by Captain R. S. Rattray in his recent anthropological study of Ashanti. The Ashanti week consists of seven days: each of these days has one, in its proper order, of the above numbers as a prefix; the result is that Fo-Sunday will recur only after forty-two days, the G.C.M. of six and seven. These forty-two days complete a cycle of time between the return of a festival. Captain Rattray learned this among the Brong portion of the Twi speakers; I learned this numeration from an Ashanti of Goaso.

But the people play a far more serious game than any of those outlined in the preceding pages. This is the game of "Wari." It seems that its extent is general throughout West Africa, and I believe the name "Wari" is almost equally widespread. However, the Ashanti claims *wari* as his own, and explains that *wari* is an Ashanti word, meaning "far," and is derived from the fact that the tokens with which it is played have "far" to go before the game is finished.

The game itself as generally played is in reality merely a reckoner by which young men learn to think quickly in figures, and I hope, if my description is clear, to show my reader that this is the case. To an onlooker not conversant with the game it seems a far more complicated matter than it really is, and has given rise to all sorts of misunderstandings, and thereby has acquired an unmerited reputation.

Wari can be played on mother earth. It is generally played on a specially constructed board. This takes the form of a small table about three feet long and eight inches wide. The sides are each provided with six cups or hollowed-out squares, and at either end of the board is a larger receptacle. These last two do not enter into the actual play; they are merely to hold the counters or tokens captured. There are only two players and each has one of these receptacles for his use.

The two sides are allotted one to each player, who owns that nearest to him. In each cup there are placed four counters. These are usually stones, cowries or seeds. There are thus forty-eight counters in all, twenty-four on each side, at the beginning of the play.

The play, being purely one of mathematical calculation, lends itself to many variations; but the commonest is as follows. A player may move the contents of any one of the receptacles on his own side, which is the one nearest to him. He thus has six squares each containing four counters. He must take all the counters in one square, and then drop one counter into each successive square to his right, following across into the squares of his opponent if necessary. His opponent does likewise, and as soon as six counters—no more, no less—are in one of his adversary's squares—the total of six being reached by his dropping one counter therein—he lifts those six from that square and puts them aside into his "prison" receptacle. If he makes six in one of his own squares, he cannot lift those.

The speed with which the game is played is extraordinary. Small children as well as adults indulge in it, and gambling over the result is only too frequent.

But a far better game than this, and one certainly worthy

of being introduced at home, is the form of *wari*—it has many other names—which is played by the people of the north. Many times have I too entered the lists, and generally, in spite of the courtesy of my opponent, have lost.

The board has thirty-six cups or squares in it. Only two players take part. Each is provided with twelve counters, either of different colour or size. Usually one has white beans and the other black beans. The board at the beginning is left entirely clear of any counters.

Each in turn is allowed to place one counter in any unoccupied square until all twenty-four have been set in place. Then he whose turn it is to play is allowed to move one of his counters to any vacant square (there are twelve left), which must be adjacent to the counter moved, but not diagonally so. If by so moving he is able to make a line of three of his own colour, he is allowed to remove any one of his opponent's counters. The latter then moves, and so the game continues until the board is cleared of one colour. It must be remembered that no counter may be removed until all the twenty-four have been set, and that only those lines made up to three after that entitle one to "huff" an opponent. A line of four or more counts for nothing, nor does the moving one of four in a row, leaving a line of three, entitle one to an enemy piece. It is only the actual making of a line which counts, and the three must be in consecutive squares.

This game always attracts a crowd of onlookers and is generally the cause of much gambling. Curiously enough the Ashanti does not take to it, although it is a far cleverer and more skilled game than his own *wari*.

Before concluding this chapter on games mention should be made of a curious play indulged in by Ashanti boys on dark nights. I have elsewhere pointed out how, owing to the height of the trees in the forest zone and the thickness of their foliage on their crests, comparatively little of the sky is visible. Yet one of their games is to collect in one hand sufficient glowing embers and to set them in order, still glowing, on the ground so that they will resemble the constellation of Orion. One can imagine that the game has to be played pretty rapidly. Orion particularly seems to be noticed by all these tribes, but the Pleiades are still more so. Other constellations do not seem to attract much notice. The Pleiades to the Ashanti and the tribes in the Protectorate are watched regularly, for by their position at their rising are determined the seasons of harvesting and sowing.

After the Dance.

Young girls removing with their hands the sweat from the dancers after a ceremonial dance by the Konne Society.

CHAPTER XVII

LANGUAGE

ONE of the first difficulties one meets with is the language question. Neither does the native speak English nor the white man native. Of course in the few towns on the coast-line, and in a still lesser number in the interior, one meets the exception to the first; to the latter one possibly meets only one exception throughout one's sojourn in West Africa.

One of the consequences has been the rise of a pidgin-English—a sort of West African Esperanto. I do not know when this pidgin first started—it cannot be of such great antiquity, since we English have not been a really important factor on the West Coast for more than a hundred and fifty years—but its very existence shows the vigour and virility of our tongue, for neither the French nor the Portuguese, both of whom have been longer on the coast than ourselves, have evolved a conversational medium, a lingua franca almost, as we have done.

This peculiar offshoot of our language is not likely to pass away. It has been very nearly rendered immortal by the publication and general reading of *Nights with Uncle Remus*; and in spite of every effort to alter it, and even to replace it with a more exact rendering of our tongue, we ourselves are constantly adding to its vocabulary.

Thus in recent years we have introduced such

expressions as cocoa-farm, cow-doctor, bush-cow, etc., all of which are vivid enough and, in spite of their inexactitude, are perfectly simple to understand. The natives on the other hand contribute as much, if not more, than we do to the growth and continuance of pidgin.

Even the local Press adds its quota, and one finds such terms as deer, tiger, prince, duke, country villa—all of which are wrongly used but yet are quite clear in their meaning, for there is neither deer nor tiger nor prince nor duke nor yet country villa in the land.

Thus it will be seen that there are two separate sources of growth—one from ourselves in an endeavour to make clear an unusual term, and one from native sources in an endeavour to apply English and European expressions to their own words indicative of their manner of living.

The great difference between the two vocabularies, English and native, and their methods of thought, tend to foster and perpetuate a pidgin language, as I suppose the Gauls spoke pidgin-Latin until eventually it became French.

In addition to the actual misuse and wrongful creation of words the idiom of pidgin is unique. It is neither native nor European, but it is certainly more nearly related to the former. This is only natural, since obviously the majority of producers and users of pidgin are natives.

In practically all books on West Africa considerable space is occupied with this question. I make no apology for following in my predecessors' footsteps, for no book dealing with the coast in a general way would be complete if this picturesque mode of expression, possibly a to-morrow's language, were ignored.

Of course not every native speaks pidgin. Many are too educated to do so. And I am afraid that too often has an unfortunate new-comer been listened to patiently as he tried his hand at pidgin, only to be answered in an English more perfectly Oxford than even he himself commands.

Of English-speaking natives there are five classes. There is the perfect speaker, who more often than not, having acquired his command—nay, super-command—of our language in England, has lost touch with his own nation. There is the larger class of native who has succeeded in passing examinations at home. Of such the archetype is Babu Jaberjee. A still larger number have reached the highest stage of education possible on the coast. They form the majority in the ranks of the so-called Intelligentia. The fourth class has been to school but has not reached that stage of advancement which fosters conceit, self-assertion, even rebellion against the conservatism of its race. And the last class, the greatest number of all, the jolly pidgin-speaking people, who have never been to school, but who have picked up our language in many a haphazard way.

This is the class that provides the largest source for the development of pidgin. They talk the cosmopolitan tongue of the steamer, camp, cantonment, workshop and servants' quarters. They bend and twist our tongue to convey their meanings, and they are far too natural to be shy or self-conscious about their achievement. On the contrary they are proud of it; and in moments of anger show scorn for their adversary by using it, thereby demonstrating to all within earshot their own superiority.

Small children, ever enthusiastic to acquire knowledge, learn from them, imitate them, and proudly greet one during the evening stroll with their " Good-morning, Sah ! " These children get themselves attached to various schools, learn a little more, and then, alas ! are handed back to the immediate service of their family before they have learned anything worthy of the name.

Thus English in a pidgin form, a true dialect as a matter of fact—if dialect means merely a local variant of a language—is a force to be considered. It is almost certainly not possible to exterminate it; it is, on the contrary, as certain that it will increase in use, develop on its own, and even in course of time weld itself to one of the local languages, and so create in the Gold Coast what Latin either directly or indirectly created with Saxon, a new and powerful language.

Everyone who visits the Gold Coast must at one time or other come across some weird examples of " English as she is spoke " of the semi-educated class. The best example I ever met with was in a Gold Coast paper, the editor of which had received it as a letter and which he published as a " Gem from our Letter-box."

GEMS FROM OUR LETTER-BOX

To the Editor.

SIR,—With reference to article which appeared . . . I beg to say something in reciprocation that the statement and particulars implied in the said article are emphatically untrue.

In elucidation to same I have been compelled to

enucleate perception that it is an undeniable fact that the inhabitants or citizens of S—— are noted for unseemly false reports; and in alleviation I must concoct that the said article is of a prejudiced nature; if not I do not exornerate any sequel of which the writer is interested.

In conclusion I must add that the signatory of the said article known as K——, as I well know is a person of an incorrigible character, idler and non-delegacy of S——; and his relative origination is of domestic maternity.

To discreminate his ill conduct, I must positively say without the least fear of hesitation that he was in the employment of H.M. Government some time ago, and through his infidelity towards his official duties, he bolted away to Lagos and after seven years he entered into criminal association, and while on the chase he embarked to Accra, there extradition warrant followed very lucky he was the evidence for prosecution against him was rendered inadequacy and was finally liberated, his conduct on the whole is non-describable.

I must again include that he was a servant to Dispenser X—— while in S——, and was feeding on him as MISTLETOE; on my taking over the duties in S——, he allures the simplicity of approach and to co-operate my intimation, I made a draw back by not getting into his association and colleague as my predecessor was with him; finally he persisted to receive free treatment and medicines for himself and families, but I always ignore his requests and I alternately inform him to pass the usual proper channel—*i.e.* to see M.O. for necessary fees to be charged. This he could not behersive to, hence he infatuate by writing unfounded article against me.

Of the languages native to the Gold Coast, there are, properly speaking, only two, and a large number of variants. There are no local words to indicate these two, and one must classify them on our own European parallels. These two languages conform roughly to the forest and the grass country: the Guinea and Sudan zones.

As a short digression it is perhaps of interest to explain what the word "Guinea" means and whence it is derived. All sorts of explanations have been given, but the most rational and most ancient is that it was a Moorish word signifying "black-man," "land of the black," in precisely the same way that the word "Sudan" is derived from the Arabic. M. Delafosse, the well-known French authority on West Africa, quotes as a proof of its ancient usage in this connexion a Moorish manuscript of the thirteenth century. The expression must have been familiar to the first Portuguese discoverers of the West Coast or Guinea Coast of Africa.

The two languages in use on the Gold Coast are not recognized as such by the natives, who divide both into scores of languages, but they draw an interesting distinction in regard to the length of time it takes to learn a new language. Thus an Ashanti from Ahafo will say: "No, I do not speak Brong." Pressed, he will say: "I can only hear one or two of the words, but if I stay here three weeks I shall be able to understand it." But the same man will say of Dagomba: "If I stay here three years I shall understand it."

The forest language is the parent tongue of the negroes, the grass language is that of the negroids. Neither could be exactly defined to-day any more than one could say what the real language of England was in the fourth century. Each country, each village had its own dialect, and some more ancient and less changed would appear totally different to the more recently formed. And as it was the case in England in those days, so it is in the Gold Coast: the language spoken by a native is a language concerned with daily requirements and is pre-eminently materialistic. Hence since daily needs are confined chiefly to local produce, local words predominate in each district, confining the original language to merely a few necessary words, but maintaining the idiom. Thus of the so-called Twi speakers one does not expect a vocabulary of the Chakosi to resemble in the least the vocabulary of a Sefwhi. The former lives in open grass country, the latter in dense forest; the former has millet and guinea-corn as his staple food-crop, the latter yams and plantains; the former uses bows and arrows, sees horses, gazelles and large antelopes, the latter uses guns, and knows neither horse, nor gazelle, nor large antelope save the bongo, which is unknown to the Chakosi. Their lives are different: the Sefwhi lives in villages, in a happy social atmosphere, free from fear of raids, murders and sudden death; the Chakosi lives in hut-groups, separate and apart, with scarce any mutual intercourse, and ever on the guard against raids, vendettas and murders.

It is natural then that these two people, though both

Twi speakers, should possess vocabularies very dissimilar; but there are a few words, however, needed by both, and these more often than not resemble each other in both languages.

But in the forest zone there are in addition commonly recognized Ga and Ewe languages, with their dialects. Ga is more or less confined to Accra and its immediate surroundings; Ewe is a coastal language which extends eastward well into Dahomey. That a very great affinity exists between these and the Twi is a fact most students will recognize. But apart from close study it stands to reason that in an area so small as that of the Gold Coast it is hardly likely that a number of really separate languages could exist side by side.

In the Sudan zone languages much more closely resemble each other, and the type so far best studied is the Moshi type, which is almost universally understood in the grass zone of the Gold Coast. It is curious how, if one takes a Dagati and asks him if he speaks Dagomba, he will absolutely deny all knowledge of that language, and yet if one observes the man carefully one will see him sit down and carry on a lively conversation in Dagati with a Dagomba-speaking Dagomba. But in this Sudanese area there is an unstudied group of dialects, spoken by the Busansi, Kassena, Isala, etc., which does not seem to resemble in the least any of the Moshi group. Personally I am convinced that these dialects are the oldest form of the language which in its newest is spoken by the Moshi. No doubt one day a philologist will trace exactly their alliance.

Thus for all matters of moment there are really only

two languages, Twi and Moshi. The former has about one million four hundred thousand speakers and the latter about six hundred thousand. But Moshi is spoken by nearly three millions on the immediate boundaries of the Gold Coast; and their people are being forced to enter the Gold Coast in large numbers every year owing to the desiccation of their own country and to its gradual exhaustion as a food-producing soil, and in addition the magnet of the wealth in the Ashanti forest acts as a powerful attraction. The French system of head taxes and hut taxes and other such taxes forces the young men to go where they can earn the money to pay them. They come, they see, and many remain.

At the present time the Gold Coast Government is establishing, at a place called Achimota, near Accra, a secondary school, which is destined no doubt to become the Oxford of West Africa. With greater boldness, as the late Right Rev. Bishop Hummel pointed out before the Commission that chose Achimota as the site for this college, the Wesleyan Mission decided on the more central Coomassie as the site for a large training school. These two must inevitably mould the future of the Gold Coast language.

Both at Achimota and at Coomassie English will be the language which the students will be taught, just as Latin was that at Oxford and Cambridge. But it stands to reason that the students will speak their own languages, be it Moshi or Twi. The latter must predominate, not only owing to the sites of the two colleges being in Twi country, but also owing to the fact that at first it will be the predominant language.

But can a native language ever rise to the level required by modern civilization to give accurate expression to thoughts so far in advance of the level of thought to which that language has risen? This is more than doubtful, and in the case of our own language it failed. And when in addition there exists the foreign language, capable of such expression yet reduced to the form and style of that native language, it would seem inevitable that the latter must be absorbed by the former and a new language, a compound of Twi and pidgin and English, be evolved.

But this is speculation and perhaps not quite in keeping with a book such as this. Yet it leads to a consideration of the genesis of these native languages, of their literature, and of their power of expansion.

One is thus brought to the realm of folklore, one of the most interesting fields of anthropological study, but one which has often been brought into disregard by the extravagances of its students. It would seem that its value lies rather in its showing how similar has been the evolution of thought among the various races of mankind than in fanciful deduction of forgotten myths in the tales natural to a nursery.

In all these African languages of the Gold Coast one is struck with this resemblance to our own childhood's stories and word-plays. Ashanti or Moshi mothers play with their babies' toes. They do not hum the story of *Ten Little Nigger Boys*, nor of the *Pig that went to Market*, but they tell how the little toe is chief and the big toe the slave that does all the work. The toes are in Twi: chief, messenger, linguist, naughty one, slave; in Moshi: idle one, messenger, thin woman, good-for-nothing, worker.

In parenthesis this is very true, for with these natives the big toe picks up small articles and is quite an active instrument in weaving and other fibre-work.

Our counting-out rhymes, such as

> " Eena, meena, mina, mo,
> Catch a monkey by his toe,
> If he holler, let him go,
> Eena, meena, mina, mo,"

have their counterparts, and are always a source of great amusement, especially among the older children, who have learned how the last number will fall. Just as " Eena, meena," etc. is the remnant of some old-time language of England, so here, in these counting-out games, we find an old disused language surviving among the children. The Krachi children count the ninth one out and use the following: *Koko*, *noyni*, *brebi*, *dembo*, *sachi*, *penye*, *jaya*, *maforo*, *pan*. It is noteworthy, however, that the tenth is usually the one counted out, as in our English form, and modern numerals used.

CHAPTER XVIII

CONUNDRUMS & PROVERBS

A FORM of literature of quite another sort, and to a large extent of educative value, is the conundrum. It is a form of game. The players, seated in a circle, propound to each in turn a conundrum, and he acquires a reputation of cleverness whose neighbour cannot answer it. The following is an example from the Bura country:

" There is on the road to Dagbon a large pot. Everyone who passes by casts therein a cowrie, yet the pot is never full."

The answer is: " That is the ear. For everyone tells it something and it never grows weary."

One from the Krachi district is: " My mother washed a new calabash and hung it up, but it never dried."

The answer is: " The cheek—because it is always moist."

A third example from the Talansi is: " My mother has seven children; the short ones are bad, but the tall ones are good."

The answer is: "The grass that grows on marshy land: short, it is useless; tall, it will make mats and roofs."

Or again: " I have a he-goat. If he does not rub against the door when I drive him home he will not go in."

To which the answer is: " There is no rain without

thunder," which is very true of the north but not of Ashanti.

Question: A locust-bean-tree has one good branch and one bad one?

Answer: Sleep and death—both brethren and apparently growing alike.

Another form of word-game is for one of the circle to say a word which has apparently no meaning at all but which has been memorized by all as the key of a proverb. Examples are numerous. The following are from the Kassena:—

1. *Question*: K i u b?

Answer: One does not make sacrifices with the leavings of a meal.

2. *Question*: C h i a w?

Answer: One does not set one's sleeping-mat upon the water.

3. *Question*: D a r a m a n d a?

Answer: A compound or house built of guinea-corn stalks.

Explanation: Equivalent to nothing, since such a house as understood by the Kassena is impossible. It neither could stand up nor could it afford shelter.

4. *Question*: Y e l a l e?

Answer: A leopard would like a ring but it has no fingers.

5. *Question*: K a r a b a k a?

Answer: One does not climb a tree with sandals on.

6. *Question*: V i l i l i c h i b?

Answer: A black ant will not make a hole as big as itself.

It is curious how easily these proverbs can be recognized among our own. But it is said that proverbs are the accumulated wisdom of the tribe. Since proverbs are usually in pairs, contradictory the one to the other, they probably are.

The language spoken by these natives has not yet reached the directness of an Anglo-Saxon character; circumlocution and parable are common. One is often struck by the delay in interpretation, which is due largely to this peculiarity. An old Nankanni came before me. He was clothed in rags and had charms and amulets all over him. In his hand he held an egg. And this is what he said:

"I am on an elephant on a hill and under a lion. If I bring a false charge against the Chief of Kandiga, may this egg fall from my hand, and as it breaks so may I die.

"The white man came out so that the poor man may have peace. I am walking about crying aloud my complaints. A poor man never lies.

"The white man has stopped the killing of people and the robbing of men. Since this house has been built (the court-house) I have never been in it. Since I am a blind man, I shall not lie.

"They have killed my son, taken my property, taken my wife's shea-butter-trees.

"You are here to help. So to you I have come."

CHAPTER XIX

WHISTLING & DRUM LANGUAGE

LONG ago it was pointed out that these languages were tonic in character, by which is meant that the tones of the syllables rather than the letters were heard, as in the South Seas one gets Savaii, Tahiti, Kahika and Hawaii, meaning the same thing and quite understandable to a native in each form. This characteristic is probably common to every language before that language is reduced to writing, and one notices it with children, who frequently, not paying attention to an order given them but hearing words, or rather tones, give their own meaning to those tones, and carry out something quite other than was intended. Particularly is this the case with the native.

These tones can of course be reproduced in many ways, and the native can talk on a frying-pan and a stick instead of with his throat and tongue muscles. It is not therefore very surprising, when one has thought it out, though at first hearing quite extraordinary, for a native to talk to his neighbour, when the latter is out of range of a shout, by whistling.

In a former book I recorded this interesting fact, but at that time did not understand how it was possible. Captain R. S. Rattray has recently published a work on Ashanti, and therein gives a careful explanation of these tones which, more than forty years ago, had been recognized among other West African negroes. From these authors one can get a clear idea of how seeming miracles are easily brought about.

Two men standing close together can carry on a conversation without much chance of the one misunderstanding the other. They can still make themselves clear by shouting when some distance apart, but the chance of a misunderstanding has slightly increased. Relying simply on tones the conversation can be carried on still further apart by whistling, but the chances of misunderstanding are greatly increased, and to a large extent the hearer has to guess the meaning.

If one is, as I am, completely unmusical, one can understand this ; for supposing I wish to whistle or hum a tune, even one so familiar as *God Save the King*, I can only do so by actually remembering the words and whistling them. Thereby I get somewhere near the tune. I think so ; others may not. But I am sufficiently close to the tune for others to recognize what I am trying to perform.

Speaking by whistling is common throughout the grass zone, and is used by the majority of boys and young men. Not all can do it, not all can understand it. Most ordinary sentences can be whistled.

When I first recorded this, many Europeans doubted, but those who have visited me have been convinced, as I took care to give them actual proofs. The usual method of proof was to tell a man to call to another to bring any little article my doubting friend might require. I showed an example at Kanjaga when this subject cropped up. There was no previous arrangement, or even any

A DANCE LEADER.

The principal dancer of the Konne Society leading the chain of youths in a ceremonial dance.

WHISTLING DISPLAY.

A Nankanni performer of a wooden whistle. At all gatherings of this tribe there are side-shows, play-acting, dancing and musical entertainments.

thought, that a demonstration of whistling would be required.

A Kassena was called, and my friend told him to whistle to another Kassena to fetch the former's pipe. The first Kassena said he could not whistle, but he called another, and this was the whistled conversation:

"Aidan! Aidan!"

"Aha?"

"Pipe. Bali's pipe—bring it."

"Pipe?"

"Aha!"

"Bali's pipe?"

"Aha! bring it."

He went inside the hut and came out and whistled: "Pipe. Where is it?"

"Cloth, pocket—cloth, right pocket."

The man went inside and brought the pipe.

One can give scores of examples of this. When I was at Krachi, some labourers were working outside my house. They were Builsa men and Lobi. Always they whistled to each other if they wanted anything, such as "Bring us some mangoes" (there are thousands of mangoes at Krachi and they bring a load of them to their work) or "Awurai says we must bring some white man's grass (*doubh*). Come!"

There is no mistaking, once one has heard it, this whistling from whistling tunes. From whistling by the mouth to whistling by reed or pipe or horn is not a long step. M. Labouret, for many years the French Commandant in the Lobi country, has written recently a studied article on this subject. He found the practice common enough among Lobi and Dagati. I myself found it among the Kussasi of the Bawku district. But now the chance of misunderstanding is much greater. Fewer people can do it and fewer understand what they hear.

It follows from the above that since the mere conveyance of tones suffices to carry on a conversation, then other instruments capable of rendering tones can be used, but with ever-decreasing chances of being correctly understood. One is brought to the well-known and often marvelled-at language of drums.

Professor Westerman long ago analysed this language and brought it to its proper place as a very limited method of conveying ideas; but unfortunately his work had no wide public. Drum language has therefore remained as one of the wonders of West Africa. In *The Gold Coast* Captain Rattray has explained the system of drum-talking with great thoroughness, and has proved how limited is its use, and he shows how in its African form it is practically valueless. I make no apology for quoting his words, for it seems a good thing to end as soon as possible the almost general belief among Europeans that the drum language is a most wonderful achievement.

"Theoretically, the expert drummer should not experience any limitations as to what he can drum, and possibly he does not; but—and this appears to be the crux of the whole question—his limitations are very real when it comes to the 'reading' of a message . . . the repertoire of Ashanti drummers consists of certain holophrases which are in constant use by all drummers. . . . Should a drummer depart, however, from one of these 'set pieces' and strike out on his own, drumming at fancy, new phrases—*i.e.* combinations of tones, etc.—then, though to himself the drum would still continue to speak, yet another drummer, who heard these new combinations for the first time, could not, I am convinced, read his message with any accuracy."

As a matter of fact, drumming is confined within very narrow limits. There are, as one would expect, warnings of danger or signals of alarm, calls to arms, news of death and, latterly, the announcement of a European's visit. But the greatest of limitations is undoubtedly distance. I do not know how far a drum can be heard. In the stillness of an African night the sound might carry a long way—perhaps six to nine miles. But only certain of the tones would reach that distance and the meaning could only be surmised. That would only be in the most favourable weather conditions. Hills and thick forest, wind and other atmospheric disturbances would all interrupt the sound waves. When one considers this, one begins to realize how little is the value of drumming in conveying meaning as practised by the natives. Extraordinary tales of news being passed across the Continent in the shortest space of time have been told. Many people believe them. But apart from their relation being after the event, there is to be reckoned the intelligent anticipation of the native and, far more important, the speed with which natives travel on foot. When one hears stories of the relief of Ladysmith or the recapture of Khartoum being sent across the Continent, one is merely in face of statements of the grossest inaccuracy, for, apart from the language difficulty — say a Yoruba drummer being heard and understood by a Ewe drummer—there could not have been any means whatsoever of rendering the words Ladysmith or Khartoum, neither of which towns was or is known to the vast majority of negroes in West Africa. It is a pity to destroy this myth; but why, after all, allow an absurd belief to survive?

CHAPTER XX

TRADE OF THE GOLD COAST

ONE cannot conclude a book concerning the Gold Coast without a few remarks on the trade of that truly wonderful colony. It is unique, I believe, in all our Empire, and every man who has the privilege of serving it, no matter in what capacity, takes pride in his service. For what are we?

We are a community of two million souls; we enjoy a trade of unmeasured value, which amounts to sixteen millions entering and passing out through our ports alone; we are a happy and contented land, and we have no direct taxation at all. We are a land of peasant proprietors and we amass our wealth through the kindness of our soil. So much for our happiness. Figures of our wealth may be boring, but they are instructive. The Gold Coast and Ashanti produce cocoa, kola, palm-nuts, palm-oil, rubber and copra, and will soon export rice, tapioca, sisal-hemp, piassava, limes, mangoes, bananas and all the rest of the wonderful gifts tropical forests give to man. The earth itself renders gold and manganese and diamonds; to-morrow it will undoubtedly yield bauxite and graphite, perhaps tin and oil. Our mineral resources are, like the soil itself, but scratched.

The grasslands of the north at present are but a market-garden for the south, and a source from which labour pours steadily to the forest zone, just as our own towns in England draw their regular recruits from the villages of the country. But their future is assured. Ground-nuts, shea-nuts, cotton, kapok, oils and fats, grains and fibres will all add immensely to our future trade.

One great problem there remains, far transcending all other problems, which, until it be solved, must hold up this certain development. That problem is population.

It has, I think, been accepted as a maxim that peasant proprietorship is not agriculturally economical. That may be. I do not discuss it. I merely know that, as typified on the Gold Coast, peasant proprietorship does show to all who pass that peasant proprietorship gives the greatest happiness to the greatest number, which, after all, economically sound or unsound, is what every Government desires.

This system, of which we all are proud, demands an inordinate amount of labour. To obtain this the population must increase. It is a problem which is being tackled from various points.

With its solution is solved also the problem of transport, for road and railway construction will be easier and cheaper when labour is more plentiful, when more food is grown.

There are other problems—each department of Government has its own to solve. The food question is one; and I often think of those in the coast towns, where the problem is sometimes acute, and of a meal I once prepared for my Chief Commissioners there. The menu was entirely of local produce and, except for sugar and coffee, nothing was from Europe.

Potage arachide

Soles frites gourounsi

Pintade Rôti
Patates Frafra
Epinard sauvage

Hanche de Venaison
Salade

Œufs de Pluvier

Champignons à la Croûte

Dessert de Fruits Sauvages

Café

That meal was one providentially provided, since I stumbled on the plovers' eggs (they were bad) and a convenient rain had produced the mushrooms. The soles were a small flat-fish found in a pond. I doubt if one could repeat the menu.

But food in the north is not always plentiful, and grim Famine often stalks near by—another problem for us to solve one day. These troubles help to make our lives out here more interesting and more satisfactory, for if one could help to solve only one of them, one's time would not have been misspent; and when one for the last time bade farewell to Eiloart's " Land of Death " it would be good-bye to one's own " Land of Happiness."

INDEX